CAROL
Ancie
&
Modern

CAROLS

Ancient
&
Modern

MUSIC EDITION

EDITED AND ARRANGED BY

MALCOLM ARCHER

Carols Ancient & Modern is published by
Hymns Ancient & Modern Ltd, a registered charity

Hymns Ancient & Modern Ltd
Third Floor, Invicta House
108-114 Golden Lane
London EC1Y 0TG

Carols Ancient & Modern Music Edition
First published September 2016

British Library Cataloguing-in-Publication Data
A catalogue record for this book is available from the British Library.

ISBN 978-1-84825-871-6

Hymns Ancient & Modern is an imprint of Hymns Ancient & Modern Ltd

Music engraving and typesetting:
Andrew Parker, Ferndown, Dorset BH22 8BB United Kingdom
Printed and bound by CPI Group (UK) Ltd, Croydon CR0 4YY

An Introduction from the Editor

When there are so many carol books on the market, one may ask the question, 'Why another one?' Well, despite the plethora of Christmas books available, many are there to serve the needs of choirs alone, and often aimed at extremely competent choirs, too. There are few books that serve church choirs, community choirs, school choirs, congregations and groups of carol singers alike. Congregations will appreciate the wider selection here, beyond the usual limited Christmas sections in many hymn books. And while there are a good number of settings in the book that choirs will enjoy, there are also many one-page carols which can be sung unaccompanied by carol singers or by a congregation accompanied by organ or piano.

Christmas is a season of the Church's year that constantly attracts new material, and composers are drawn to the magic of Christmas texts, and we all like to ring the changes from year to year as well as enjoy our old favourites. *Carols Ancient & Modern* has all the old favourites, but also some exciting new arrangements which are singable, fresh and not over-challenging. So, in addition to the traditional tune for 'Away in a manger', we include a new arrangement of the American tune by James Murray, (arranged here by Oliver Tarney). There is also a new setting of the words 'When righteous Joseph wedded was', and a new four-part arrangement (with organ) of Warlock's delightful setting of 'Adam lay ybounden'. We have also welcomed some modern texts, including Susan Sayers' words of 'The Mother of Jesus' sung to a traditional French melody. In fact, this collection contains traditional carols from all over the globe.

We have extended the season of Christmas to include Advent and Epiphany, and have also included carols which may be sung for a Christingle service.

We believe this is an exciting new Christmas resource for all to enjoy, and Hymns Ancient & Modern are proud to add this to their list of fine publications. We hope this book will be useful, varied and celebratory, and that it will spice up your enjoyment of Christmas music.

Malcolm Archer, 2016

ADVENT

A - dam lay y-bound-en, bound - en in a bond; _
four thou - sand win - ter thought he not too long. And
All for an ap - ple, an ap - ple that he took,
all was for an ap - ple, an ap - ple that he took,
as clerk - es find - en writ-ten in their book.

Music: BORIS ORD (1897–1961)

ADVENT

British Library, Sloane MS 2593, ff10v-11, modernised
15th century or earlier

Allegretto

A-dam lay y-bound-en, bound-en in a bond; four thou-sand win-ter thought he not too long. And all was for an ap-ple, an ap-ple that he took, as clerk - es find - en writ-ten in their book. Ne had the ap-ple ta-ken been, the

Music: PHILIP ARNOLD HESELTINE, (PETER WARLOCK) (1894–1930)
adapted by MALCOLM ARCHER (b. 1952)

ADVENT

apple taken been, ne had never our lady a-been heavene queen.

Blessed be the time that apple taken was;

therefore we moun singen: Deo gratias!

British Library, Sloane MS 2593, ff10v-11, modernised
15th century or earlier

ANGEL VOICES

85 85 87

Music: EDWIN GEORGE MONK (1819–1900)

ADVENT

For lighting candles on an Advent wreath

Advent 1

1 Advent candles tell their story
    as we watch and pray;
longing for the Day of Glory,
    'Come, Lord, soon,' we say.
Pain and sorrow, tears and sadness
    changed for gladness on that Day.

Advent 2

2 Prophet voices loudly crying,
    making pathways clear;
glimpsing glory, self-denying,
    calling all to hear.
Through their message — challenged, shaken —
    hearts awaken: God is near!

Advent 3

3 John the Baptist, by his preaching
    and by water poured,
brought to those who heard his teaching
    news of hope restored:
'Keep your vision strong and steady,
    and be ready for the Lord.'

Advent 4

4 Mary's gift beyond all telling
    we recall today:
Son of God within her dwelling,
    born to show the way.
Who could guess the final story?
    — cross and glory; Easter Day!

Christmas Day

5 Advent candles tell their story
    on this Christmas Day.
Those who waited for God's glory:
    they prepared the way.
Christ is with us: loving, giving,
    in us living, here today!

MARK EAREY (b. 1965)

Music: RICHARD RUNCIMAN TERRY (1865–1938)

ADVENT

As Joseph was a-walking,
he heard an angel sing:
'This night is born to Mary
our heav'nly King.'

1 He neither shall be born
   in house nor in hall,
   nor in a place of paradise
   but in an oxen stall.
   Nowell, nowell.

2 He neither shall be covered
   in clothing rich and rare,
   but in the simple linen
   which all the babies wear.
   Nowell, nowell.

3 He neither shall be rocked
   in silver nor in gold,
   but in the wooden manger
   which rocks upon the mould.
   Nowell, nowell.

Cherry Tree Carol, part ii, English traditional
collected by Hone in *Ancient Mysteries Described,*
1823and elsewhere.
adapted by MALCOLM ARCHER (*b.* 1952)

CROSS OF JESUS   87 87

Music: JOHN STAINER (1840–1901)
    from *The Crucifixion,* 1887

1   Come, thou long-expected Jesus,
        born to set thy people free;
    from our fears and sins release us;
        let us find our rest in thee.

2   Israel's strength and consolation,
        hope of all the earth thou art;
    dear desire of every nation,
        joy of every longing heart.

3   Born thy people to deliver;
        born a child and yet a king;
    born to reign in us for ever;
        now thy gracious kingdom bring.

4   By thy own eternal Spirit,
        rule in all our hearts alone:
    by thy all-sufficient merit,
        raise us to thy glorious throne.

CHARLES WESLEY (1707–1788)*

CONDITOR ALME   LM

A - men. ____

Music: Mode iv
      harmonised by MICHAEL FLEMING (1928–2006)

1   Creator of the stars of night,
     thy people's everlasting light,
     O Jesu, Saviour of us all,
     regard thy servants when they call.

2   Thou, grieving at the bitter cry
     of all creation doomed to die,
     didst come to save a ruined race
     with healing gifts of heavenly grace.

2   Thous camest, Bridegroom of the bride,
     as drew the world to evening-tide,
     proceeding from a virgin shrine,
     the Son of Man, yet Lord divine.

3   At thy great name, exalted now,
     all knees must bend, all hearts must bow,
     and things in heaven and earth shall own
     that thou art Lord and King alone.

4   To thee, O holy One, we pray,
     our judge in that tremendous day,
     preserve us, while we dwell below,
     from every onslaught of the foe.

5   All praise, eternal Son, to thee,
     whose advent sets thy people free,
     whom with the Father we adore,
     and Spirit blest, for evermore. Amen.

Latin hymn, 9th century
translated by JOHN MASON NEALE (1818–1866)
Adapted by Compilers of *New English Hymnal,* 1986

Music: 14th-century Advent carol
    arranged by MALCOLM ARCHER (*b.* 1952)

1 Gabriel to Mary came,
 a gentle message bare he;
deep in awe the Maiden bowed
 to hear him say, 'Hail, Mary.'
There, heav'n and earth received his call,
'Hail, hail thou queen of virgins all;
  thou, yet undefiled,
  shalt bear a child
  of sov'reign grace,
 to comfort all mankind;
thou shalt bear him, Lord and God of all,
 to save our human race.'

2 'How shall this befall,' said she,
 'to me, a virgin lowly?
How can I deny the vows
 that bind me to be holy?'
Then said the angel, 'Maid, believe
God's Holy Ghost shall this achieve,
  so be not afraid,
  but now rejoice,
  rejoice indeed
 for ever in his sight;
for thy trust shall be in his mercy,
 by God's especial might.'

3 Then bespoke the Maid again,
 within her lowly bower,
'I the humble handmaid am
 of God's almighty power.
So to his messenger most blest,
bearing in secret his behest,
  I will answer
  and obey with love
  and holy joy
 the tidings I have heard;
for I now before thy holy will,
 according to thy word.'

Turn over for v.4.

7 Adaptation: © Campion Press Permission applied for.

CAROLS ANCIENT & MODERN

4   Maid and Mother of us all,
      who bore the gift God gave us,
praise we now in earth and heav'n
      thy Son who came to save us.
Pray thou thy child, the Lord of love,
that he may hear in heav'n above,
      and may succour
      and redeem us
      by his holy birth,
and save us when we roam;
that by his good grace we may find place
    in heaven's eternal home.

Angelus ad Virginem, 14th-century Advent carol
paraphrased ELIZABETH POSTON (1905–1987)

Music: African-American Spiritual melody
arranged by OLIVER TARNEY (*b.* 1984)

Go tell it on the mountain,
over the hills and everywhere;
go tell it on the mountain
that Jesus Christ is born!

1   While shepherds kept their watching
    o'er silent flocks by night,
behold, throughout the heavens
    there shone a holy light.

2   The shepherds feared and trembled,
    when lo! above the earth,
rang out the angels chorus
    that hailed the Saviour's birth.

3   Down in a lowly manger
    the humble Christ was born,
and God sent us salvation
    that blessèd Christmas morn.

JOHN WESLEY WORK (*c.*1871–1925)
based on African-American Spritual,
early 19th century

Music: Melody from Matteo Coferati's
Corona di Sacre Canzoni o Laude Spirituali, 1689
harmonised by CHARLES WOOD (1866–1926)

1   Hail, blessèd virgin Mary!
        For so, when he did meet thee,
    spake mighty Gabriel, and thus we greet thee.
    Come weal, come woe, our song shall never vary:
        Hail, blessèd virgin Mary!
        Hail, blessèd virgin Mary!

2   Ave, ave Maria!
        To gladden priest and people
    the Angelus shall ring from every steeple
    to sound his virgin birth, Allelu-i-a!
        Ave, ave Maria!
        Ave, ave Maria!

3   Archangels chant, 'Osanna!'
        and 'Holy, holy, holy!'
    before the infant born of thee, thou lowly
    aye-maiden child of Joachim and Anna.
        Archangels chant, 'Osanna!'
        Archangels chant, 'Osanna!'

GEORGE RATCLIFFE WOODWARD (1848–1934)

MERTON 87 87

Descant (v. 5)

Music: WILLIAM HENRY MONK (1823–1889)
descant by JOHN BARNARD (*b.* 1948)

1 Hark, a thrilling voice is sounding;
       'Christ is nigh,' it seems to say;
   'cast away the dreams of darkness,
       O ye children of the day.'

2 Wakened by the solemn warning,
       let the earth-bound soul arise;
   Christ, her Sun, all ill dispelling,
       shines upon the morning skies.

3 Lo, the Lamb, so long expected,
       comes with pardon down from heaven;
   let us haste, with tears of sorrow,
       one and all to be forgiven;

4 That when next he comes with glory,
       and the world is wrapped in fear,
   with his mercy he may shield us,
       and with words of love draw near.

5 Honour, glory, might, and blessing
       to the Father and the Son,
   with the everlasting Spirit,
       while eternal ages run.

EDWARD CASWALL (1814–1878)*
based on *Vox clama ecce intonat,*
(Latin, 5th or 6th century)

Music: English traditional carol
Collected by DAVIES GILBERT, (DAVIES GIDDY) (1767–1839)
arranged by MALCOLM ARCHER (*b.* 1952)

11   Arrangement: © Malcolm Archer / Hymns Ancient & Modern Ltd <www.hymnsam.co.uk>

1   Joseph was an old man
         and an old man was he,
      when he married Mary
         in the land of Galilee.

2   And as they were walking ⌣
         through an orchard so good,
      where were cherries and berries
         as red as any blood —

3   O then bespoke Mary,
         with words both meek and mild,
      'Pluck me one cherry, Joseph;
         for that I am with child.'

4   'Go to the tree, Mary,
         and it shall bow to thee;
      and you shall gather cherries
         by one, by two, by three.'

5   Then bowed down the highest tree ⌣
         unto our Lady's hand;
      'See,' Mary cried, 'see, Joseph,
         I have cherries at command.'

6   'O eat your cherries, Mary,
         O eat your cherries, now;
      O eat your cherries, Mary,
         that grow upon the bough.'

7   Then Mary plucked a cherry,
         as red as any blood,
      then Mary went she homewards ⌣
         all with her heavy load.

Cherry Tree Carol, part ii, English traditional
collected by Hone in *Ancient Mysteries Described,* 1823

HELMSLEY   87 87 47 extended

Music: Melody adapted from John Wesley's
          Select Hymns with Tunes Annext, 1765
          descant by MALCOLM ARCHER (*b.* 1952)

1 Lo, he comes with clouds descending,
      once for favoured sinners slain;
   thousand thousand saints attending
      swell the triumph of his train:
         Alleluia!
      God appears on earth to reign.

2 Every eye shall now behold him
      robed in dreadful majesty;
   those who set at naught and sold him,
      pierced and nailed him to the Tree,
         deeply wailing,
      shall the true Messiah see.

3 Those dear tokens of his passion
      still his dazzling body bears,
   cause of endless exultation
      to his ransomed worshippers:
         with what rapture
      gaze we on those glorious scars!

4 Yea, Amen, let all adore thee,
      high on thine eternal throne;
   Saviour, take the power and glory,
      claim the kingdom for thine own:
         Alleluia!
      Thou shalt reign, and thou alone.

CHARLES WESLEY (1707–1788)
and JOHN CENNICK (1718–1755)

The fifth line of each verse is sung three times.

Turn over for arrangement of v.4 with descant.

4 Yea,__ A - men, let all_____ a - dore__ thee,

high__ on__ thine e - ter - nal__ throne; Sa - viour,

take the power_____ and glo - ry, claim__ the king - dom

for__ thine__ own: Al - le - lu - ia! Al-

ADVENT

-le-lu - - - ia! Al - - - le - lu - -

-ia! Thou shalt reign, _ and _ thou a - - - lone.

CHRIST BE OUR LIGHT

1 Long-ing for light,____ we wait in dark-ness. Long-ing for

truth,____ we turn to you. Make us your own,____

your ho-ly peo-ple, light for the world to see.____

Descant *(last verse)*

Christ, be our light! Shine out through the

Refrain

Christ, be our light! Shine in our hearts. Shine through the

Music: BERNADETTE FARRELL *(b.* 1957*)*

ADVENT

dark, shine!___ Christ,_ be our light! Shine in your

dark - - ness. Christ, be our light! Shine in your

church ga-thered to - day.___

church ga-thered to - day.___

Fine

2   Longing for peace, our world is troubled.
Longing for hope, many despair.
Your word alone has power to save us.
    Make us your living voice.

3   Longing for food, many are hungry.
Longing for water, many still thirst.
Make us your bread, broken for others,
    shared until all are fed.

4   Longing for shelter, many are homeless.
Longing for warmth, many are cold.
Make us your building, sheltering others,
    walls made of living stone.

5   Many the gifts, many the people,
many the hearts that yearn to belong.
Let us be servants to one another,
    making your kingdom come.

BERNADETTE FARRELL (b. 1957)

VENI EMMANUEL

88 88 and refrain

Music: Melody 'adapted from a French Missal' by
THOMAS HELMORE (1811–1890)
harmonised by NOËL TREDINNICK (b. 1949)
descant by DAVID ILIFF (b. 1939)

1   O come, O come, Emmanuel,
and ransom captive Israel,
that mourns in lonely exile here,
until the Son of God appear:

     Rejoice! Rejoice! Emmanuel
     shall come to thee, O Israel.

2   O come, thou Rod of Jesse, free
thine own from Satan's tyranny;
from depths of hell thy people save,
and give them victory o'er the grave:

3   O come, thou Dayspring, come and cheer
our spirits by thine advent here;
disperse the gloomy clouds of night,
and death's dark shadows put to flight:

4   O come, thou Key of David, come,
and open wide our heavenly home;
make safe the way that leads on high,
and close the path to misery:

5   O come, O come, thou Lord of Might,
who to thy tribes, on Sinai's height,
in ancient times didst give the law
in cloud and majesty and awe:

JOHN MASON NEALE (1818–1866)[*]
translated from Latin Advent Antiphons

WINCHESTER NEW

Music: Adapted from a chorale in *Musicalisches Hand-Buch*, Hamburg, 1690

1   On Jordan's bank the Baptist's cry
        announces that the Lord is nigh;
    awake and hearken, for he brings
        glad tidings from the King of kings.

2   Then cleansed be every breast from sin;
        make straight the way for God within;
    prepare we in our hearts a home,
        where such a mighty guest may come.

3   For thou art our salvation, Lord,
        our refuge and our great reward;
    without thy grace we waste away,
        like flowers that wither and decay.

4   To heal the sick stretch out thine hand,
        and bid the fallen sinner stand;
    shine forth, and let thy light restore
        earth's own true loveliness once more.

5   All praise, eternal Son, to thee
        whose advent sets thy people free,
    whom with the Father we adore,
        and Holy Ghost for evermore.

Jordanis oras praevia
CHARLES COFFIN (1676–1749)
translated by JOHN CHANDLER (1806–1876)*

BESANÇON CAROL

Music: French traditional carol
harmonised by BARRY ROSE (*b.* 1934)

1   People, look east to see at last
         hopes fulfilled from ages past:
     now in the promise of the morning,
         see, a brighter day is dawning,
     rich with the visions long foretold,
         prophets' dreams from days of old.

2   God reaffirms the gracious call:
         words of welcome meant for all;
     comfort enough for all our sorrows;
         justice shaping new tomorrows.
     Mercy bears fruit in lives restored,
         freed to praise and serve the Lord.

3   Now, with the coming of the light,
         darkest fears are put to flight;
     see how the clouds of gloom are clearing,
         blown aside by hope's appearing.
     Jesus, the Light of all our days,
         comes and sets our hearts ablaze.

4   Born of our race, a child so small —
         hail the promised Lord of all!
     Nailed to a cross for our salvation,
         he shall rule God's new creation.
     Lift up your eyes, and look again:
         see, he comes in power to reign!

MARTIN LECKEBUSCH (b. 1962)

GABRIEL'S MESSAGE   10 10 12 7 3

1 The an-gel Ga-bri-el from hea-ven came,
his wings as drift-ed snow, his eyes as flame:
'All hail,' said he, 'thou low-ly maid-en Ma - - - ry,
most high-ly fa-voured la - dy!' Glo - - - - ri - - a!

Music: Basque traditional carol
      arranged by CHARLES EDGAR PETTMAN (1866–1943)

1   The Angel Gabriel from heaven came,
      his wings as drifted snow, his eyes as flame;
   'All hail,' said he, 'thou lowly maiden Mary,
        most highly favoured lady!'
          Gloria!

2   'For known a blessèd Mother thou shalt be,
      all generations laud and honour thee,
 thy son shall be Emmanuel, by seers foretold;
        most highly favoured lady!'
          Gloria!

3   Then gentle Mary meekly bowed her head,
      'To me be as it pleaseth God,' she said,
   'My soul shall laud and magnify his holy name':
        most highly favoured lady!
          Gloria!

4   Of her, Emmanuel, the Christ was born
      in Bethlehem, all on a Christmas morn,
 and Christian folk throughout the world will ever say
        'Most highly favoured lady!'
          Gloria!

Birjina gaztetto bat zegoen (Basque Carol)
paraphrased by SABINE BARING-GOULD (1834–1924)

Music: West of England traditional carol melody
harmonised by MALCOLM ARCHER (*b.* 1952)

1 The Lord at first did Adam make
  out of the dust and clay,
and in his nostrils breathèd life,
  e'en as the Scriptures say.
And then in Eden's paradise
  he placèd him to dwell,
that he within it should remain
  to dress and keep it well.

  Now let good Christians all begin
   an holy life to live,
  and to rejoice and merry be,
   for this is Christmas Eve.

2 And then within the garden he
  commanded was to stay,
and unto him in commandment
  these words the Lord did say:
the fruit which in the garden grows
  to thee shall be for meet,
except the tree in the midst thereof,
  of which thou shalt not eat.

3 For in the day that thou shalt eat,
  or do it them come nigh;
for if that thou doth eat thereof
  then surely thou shalt die.
but Adam he did take no heed
  unto that only thing,
but did transgress God's holy law,
  and so was wrapt in sin.

4 Now mark the goodness of the Lord
  which he for mankind bore,
his mercy soon he did extend,
  lost man for to restore;
and then for to redeem our souls
  from death and hellish thrall,
he said his own dear son should be
  the Saviour of us all.

West of England carol as in *Some ancient Christmas Carols*, 1822
Collected by DAVIES GILBERT, (DAVIES GIDDY) (1767–1839)

Music: JOHN JOUBERT (b. 1927)

ADVENT

-da. By that rose we may well see there

-da. By that rose we may well see there

-da. By that rose we may well see there

-da. By that rose we may well see there

be one God in Per - sons Three: Pa - -

be one God in Per - - - sons Three: Pa - -

(prominent)

be one God in Per - sons Three. Pa - -

be one God in Per - sons Three: Pa - -

ADVENT

1   There is no rose of such virtue
as is the rose that bare Jesu:
Alleluia.

2   For in this rose contained was
heaven and earth in little space:
Res miranda.

3   By that rose we may well see
there be one God in Persons Three:
Pares forma.

4   Then leave we all this worldly mirth,
and follow we this joyous birth:
Transeamus.

English early 15th-century carol

Music: English traditional carol
    arranged by RALPH VAUGHAN WILLIAMS (1872–1958)

1   This is the truth sent from above,
the truth of God, the God of love;
therefore don't turn me from your door,
but hearken all both rich and poor.

2   The first thing that I will relate
that God at first did man create;
the next thing which to you I tell —
woman was made with him to dwell.

3   Thus we were heirs to endless woes
till God the Lord did interpose;
and so a promise soon did run:
that he'd redeem us by his Son.

4   And at this season of the year
our blest Redeemer did appear,
and here did live, and here did preach,
and many thousands he did teach.

5   Thus he in love to us behaved,
to show us how we must be saved;
and if you want to know the way,
be pleased to hear what he did say.

A Good Christmas Box, 1847

1 When right-teous Jo - seph wed-ded was to _ Ma - ry, bless-ed maid, the an - gel Ga - briel came from heav'n and to the vir - gin said: 'Hail

bless - ed Ma - ry full of grace, the Lord re-main on thee; thou shalt con-ceive and bear a son, our Sa-viour for to

Music: Melody from Davies Gilbert's *Some Ancient Christmas Carols,* 1822
arranged by MALCOLM ARCHER (b. 1952)

Ah____

Ma-ry and her hus-band kind to-ge-ther did re-main un-

Ah____

As

Ah____

-til the time of Je-sus' birth, as scrip-ture doth make plain.

Ah____

mo-ther, wife, and vir-tuous maid, our Sa-viour sweet con-ceived; and

Ah____

ADVENT

in due time to bring us him, of whom we were be - reaved. Then

Ah _____

Then

sing you all, both great and small, _ No- well, No-well, No - well! _ We

may re-joice to hear the voice _____ of the an-gel Ga-bri - el.

hear the voice of the an-gel Ga-bri - el.

Man.

ADVENT

Ah _____

spi-rit blest, that with his might did quell the world, the flesh, and

(8' reed)

Then sing you all,   both

by his death   did con-quer death and   hell.

1   When righteous Joseph wedded was
      to Mary, blessèd maid,
    the angel Gabriel came from heav'n,
      and to the Virgin said:
    'Hail, blessed Mary, full of grace,
      the Lord remain on thee;
    thou shalt conceive and bear a son,
      our Saviour for to be.'

> *Then sing you all, both great and small,*
>   *Nowell, Nowell, Nowell!*
> *We may rejoice to hear the voice*
>   *of the angel Gabriel.*

2   Thus Mary and her husband kind
      together did remain
    until the time of Jesus' birth,
      as scripture doth make plain.
    As mother, wife and virtuous maid,
      our Saviour sweet conceived;
    and in due time to bring us him,
      of whom we were bereaved.

3   Sing praises all, both old and young,
      to him that wrought such things;
    and all without the means of man
      sent us the King of kings,
    who is of such a spirit blest
      that by his might did quell
    the world, the flesh, and by his death
      did conquer death and hell.

West of England carol as in *Some ancient Christmas Carols*, 1822
Collected by DAVIES GILBERT, (DAVIES GIDDY) (1767–1839)

CHRISTMAS

ES IST EIN ROS ENTSPRUNGEN

76 76 and refrain

Music: German carol melody
harmonised by MICHAEL PRAETORIUS (1571–1621)

1   A great and mighty wonder,
     a full and holy cure!
   the Virgin bears the Infant
     with virgin-honour pure:

      Repeat the hymn again:
      'To God on high be glory,
      and peace on earth to men.'

2   The Word becomes incarnate,
     and yet remains on high;
   and cherubim sing anthems
     to shepherds from the sky:

3   While thus they sing your Monarch,
     those bright angelic bands,
   rejoice, ye vales and mountains,
     ye oceans, clap your hands:

4   Since all he comes to ransom,
     by all be he adored,
   the Infant born in Bethl'em,
     the Saviour and the Lord:

Μέγα καὶ παράδοξον θαῦμα τετέλεσται
ST GERMANUS (*c.*639–*c.*734)
translated by JOHN MASON NEALE (1818–1866)

A VIRGIN MOST PURE

11 11 11 11 and refrain

Music: Melody from Davies Gilbert's *Some Ancient Christmas Carols,* 1822
  harmonised by CHARLES WOOD (1866–1926)
  from *Cowley Carol Book* Second Series 1919

1   A virgin most pure, as the prophets do tell,
hath brought forth a baby, as it hath befell;
to be our Redeemer from death, hell and sin,
which Adam's transgession hath wrappèd us in.

Aye, and therefore be merry,
rejoice, and be you merry, set sorrow aside!
Christ Jesus our Saviour was born at this tide.

2   In Bethlehem Jewry a city there was,
where Joseph and Mary together did pass,
and there to be taxèd with many one mo,
for Caesar commanded the same should be so.

3   But when they had entered the city so fair,
the number of people so mighty was there
that Joseph and Mary, whose substance was small,
could find in the inn there no lodging at all.

4   Then they were constrained in a stable to lie,
where horses and asses they used for to tie;
their lodging so simple, they took it no scorn,
but against the next morning our Saviour was born.

5   The King of all kings to this world being brought,
small store of fine linen to wrap him was sought;
when Mary had swaddled her young son so sweet,
within an ox-manger she laid him to sleep.

6   Then God sent an angel from heaven so high
to certain poor shepherds in fields where they lie,
and bade them no longer in sorrow to stay,
because that our Saviour was born on this day.

7   Then presently after the shepherds did spy
a number of angels that stood in the sky;
they joyfully talkèd and sweetly did sing,
'To God be all glory, our heavenly King!'

West of England carol as in *Some ancient Christmas Carols,* 1822
Collected by DAVIES GILBERT, (DAVIES GIDDY) (1767–1839)

WARUM SOLLT ICH MICH DENN GRÄMEN   8336 D

Music: Melody by JOHANN GEORG EBELING (1637–1676)
in *P. Gerhardt's Geistliche Andachten mit neuen Melodien* Berlin 1666-7
harmonised by GEORGE RATCLIFFE WOODWARD (1848–1934)
in *Songs of Syon* 1910

1   All my heart this night rejoices,
        as I hear,
        far and near,
   sweetest angel voices;
   'Christ is born,' their choirs are singing,
        till the air
        everywhere
   now with joy is ringing.

2   Hark! a voice from yonder manger,
        soft and sweet,
        doth entreat,
   'Flee from woe and danger;
   brethren come, from all doth grieve you
        you are freed,
        all you need
   I will surely give you.'

3   Come then, let us hasten yonder;
        here let all,
        great and small,
   kneel in awe and wonder,
   love him who with love is yearning;
        hail the Star
        that from far
   bright with hope is burning!

4   Thee, dear Lord, with heed I'll cherish,
        live to thee,
        and with thee,
   dying shall not perish;
   but shall dwell with thee for ever,
        far on high,
        in the joy
   that can alter never.

PAUL GERHARDT (1607–1676)
translated by CATHERINE WINKWORTH (1827–1878)*

IRIS

87 87 47

Music: French traditional carol
  harmonised by MARTIN SHAW (1875–1958)

1   Angels from the realms of glory,
        wing your flight o'er all the earth;
    ye who sang creation's story
        now proclaim Messiah's birth:

        Gloria in excelsis Deo.
        Gloria in excelsis Deo.

2   Shepherds in the field abiding,
        watching o'er your flocks by night,
    God with us is now residing;
        yonder shines the infant Light:

3   Sages, leave your contemplations;
        brighter visions beam afar;
    seek the great Desire of Nations;
        ye have seen his natal star:

4   Though an infant now we view him,
        he shall fill his Father's throne,
    gather all the nations to him;
        every knee shall then bow down:

JAMES MONTGOMERY (1771–1854)
Refrain from French traditional carol
from *Iris,* 1816 and *The Christmas Box,* 1825

CRADLE SONG   11 11 11 11

Music: Melody by WILLIAM JAMES KIRKPATRICK (1838–1921)
Around the World with Christmas, 1895
harmonised by DAVID WILLCOCKS (1919–2015)

1   Away in a manger, no crib for a bed,
      the little Lord Jesus laid down his sweet head;
   the stars in the bright sky looked down where he lay,
      the little Lord Jesus asleep on the hay.

2   The cattle are lowing, the baby awakes,
      but little Lord Jesus no crying he makes.
   I love thee, Lord Jesus! Look down from the sky,
      and stay by my side until morning is nigh.

3   Be near me, Lord Jesus; I ask thee to stay
      close by me for ever, and love me, I pray.
   Bless all the dear children in thy tender care,
      and fit us for heaven, to live with thee there.

AUTHOR UNKNOWN
vv. 1, 2 *Little children's book,* Philadelphia, 1885
v. 3 *Vineyard Songs,* C. H. Gabriel, 1892

MANGER SCENE (MUELLER (Murray)) 11 11 11 11

Music: JAMES RAMSEY MURRAY (1841–1905)
adapted by OLIVER TARNEY (*b.* 1984)

1 Away in a manger, no crib for a bed,
  the little Lord Jesus laid down his sweet head;
 the stars in the bright sky looked down where he lay,
  the little Lord Jesus asleep on the hay.

2 The cattle are lowing, the baby awakes,
  but little Lord Jesus no crying he makes.
 I love thee, Lord Jesus! Look down from the sky,
  and stay by my side until morning is nigh.

3 Be near me, Lord Jesus; I ask thee to stay
  close by me for ever, and love me, I pray.
 Bless all the dear children in thy tender care,
  and fit us for heaven, to live with thee there.

AUTHOR UNKNOWN
vv. 1, 2 *Little children's book,* Philadelphia, 1885
v. 3 *Vineyard Songs,* C. H. Gabriel, 1892

Music: Dans cette étable based on 18th-century French carol
CHARLES-FRANÇOIS GOUNOD (1818–1893)

2   God comes in weakness,
and to our world for love
    descends with meekness
from realms of light above.
This child shall heal our wrong,
for sorrow give a song,
and hope in place of bleakness;
for nothing is so strong
    as God in weakness.

3   Now night is ended!
The chasm that divides
    at last is mended,
and God with us abides.
For on this happy morn
new glory wakes the dawn;
the Sun is high ascended —
to us a child is born,
    and night is ended!

MICHAEL PERRY (1942–1996)
after Esprit Fléchier 1632- 1710

BUNESSAN   55 53 D

Music: Gaelic traditional melody
    arranged by MALCOLM ARCHER (b. 1952)

Leanabh an àigh

1   Child in the manger,
    infant of Mary;
    outcast and stranger,
        Lord of all!
    Child who inherits
    all our transgressions,
    all our demerits
        on him fall.

2   Once the most holy
    child of salvation
    gently and lowly
        lived below;
    now, as our glorious
    mighty Redeemer,
    see him victorious
        o'er each foe.

3   Prophets foretold him,
    infant of wonder;
    angels behold him
        on his throne;
    worthy our Saviour
    of all their praises;
    happy for ever
        are his own.

Gaelic carol
MARY MACDONALD (1789–1872)
translated by LACHLAN MACBEAN (1853–1931)

Music: French Lorrain carol melody
arranged by OLIVER TARNEY (b. 1984)

Child of heaven born on earth —
let the music sound his praises;
Child of heaven born on earth —
sing to greet the Saviour's birth!

1   Christ, our hope, our joy, appears —
for this time we have been waiting;
Christ, our hope, our joy, appears —
promise of a thousand years.
Child of heaven born on earth —
let the music sound his praises;
Child of heaven born on earth —
sing to greet the Saviour's birth!

2   Cold within a lowly cave —
tightly wrapped in manger lying;
cold within a lowly cave
is our God who stoops to save.
Child of heaven born on earth —
let the music sound his praises;
Child of heaven born on earth —
sing to greet the Saviour's birth!

3   Jesus, king and mighty one,
gentle babe in Mary's keeping;
Jesus, King and mighty one,
come to make our hearts your throne!
Child of heaven born on earth —
let the music sound his praises;
Child of heaven born on earth —
sing to greet the Saviour's birth!

French Lorrain carol *Il est né le divin Enfant,*
19th-century or earlier.
translated by MICHAEL PERRY (1942–1996)

YORKSHIRE

10 10 10 10 10 10

Music: JOHN WAINWRIGHT (1723–1768)
harmony based on WILLIAM HENRY MONK (1823–1889)

1 Christians, awake! salute the happy morn,
    whereon the Saviour of the world was born;
rise to adore the mystery of love,
    which hosts of angels chanted from above:
with them the joyful tidings first begun
    of God incarnate and the Virgin's Son.

2 Then to the watchful shepherds it was told,
    who heard the angelic herald's voice, 'Behold,
I bring good tidings of a Saviour's birth
    to you and all the nations upon earth:
this day hath God fulfilled his promised word,
    this day is born a Saviour, Christ the Lord.'

*3 He spake; and straightway the celestial choir
    in hymns of joy, unknown before, conspire;
the praises of redeeming love they sang,
    and heaven's whole orb with alleluias rang:
God's highest glory was their anthem still,
    peace upon earth, and unto men good will.

4 To Bethl'em straight the enlightened shepherds ran,
    to see the wonder God had wrought for man,
and found, with Joseph and the blessèd Maid,
    her Son, the Saviour, in a manger laid:
then to their flocks, still praising God, return,
    and their glad hearts with holy rapture burn.

*5 O may we keep and ponder in our mind
    God's wondrous love in saving lost mankind;
trace we the babe, who hath retrieved our loss,
    from his poor manger to his bitter cross;
tread in his steps, assisted by his grace,
    till man's first heavenly state again takes place.

6 Then may we hope, the angelic hosts among,
    to sing, redeemed, a glad triumphal song:
he that was born upon this joyful day
    around us all his glory shall display;
saved by his love, incessant we shall sing
    eternal praise to heaven's almighty King.

JOHN BYROM (1692–1763)*

♩. = 66

mf

1 Christ - ians, make a joy - ful sound, sing to all the
2 Migh - ty God, Em - man - u - el— prince of whom the
3 Come, you choirs, with glad - ness sing, in - stru - ments of
4 Love is here to seek and save— hea - ven's mas - ter

world a - round: he is in a man - ger found, the
pro - phets tell, child an - nounced by Ga - bri - el, the
mu - sic bring— ea - ger to pro - claim the King, the
as a slave: God so loved the world he gave the

ho - ly one, the in - fant son of Ma - ry.

Let the peo - ple join to say that Christ the Lord is

Music: German melody in Moosburg gradual   *c.* 1360
      arranged by JOHN BARNARD (*b.* 1948)

MICHAEL PERRY (1942–1996)
Based on *Resonet in laudibus*, 14th century or earlier

Come to Beth - le-hem and see the new - born King,
come and lay your heart be - fore him while you sing:
he, the God of earth and hea - ven, Lord of all,
lies with - in the man - ger of an ox - 's stall;

He, the Lord of all be - fore our race be - gan,
loves to be and call him - self the Son of Man;
ho - ly Ma - ry, vir - gin mo - ther, gave him birth –
see her meek - ly kneel be - fore him on the earth.

Music: PHILIP ARNOLD HESELTINE, (PETER WARLOCK) (1894–1930)
     Pieds en l'Air from the *Capriol Suite*
     arranged by DAVID ILIFF (*b.* 1939)

born _ of God, the Fa - ther in __ the bliss a - bove,
Let _ us kneel with her __ and lov - ing - ly __ a - dore

born _ a ba - by in __ a sta - ble for __ our love.
Christ, her son, our God _ and King _ for ev - er - more!

If it is wished to sing the harmony, the lower voices should hum or sing to '*Ah*'.

1   Come to Bethlehem and see the newborn King,
come and lay your heart before him while you sing:
he, the God of earth and heaven, Lord of all,
lies within the manger of an ox's stall;
born of God, the Father in the bliss above,
born a baby in a stable for our love.

2   He, the Lord of all before our race began,
loves to be and call himself the Son of Man;
holy Mary, virgin mother, gave him birth —
see her meekly kneel before him on the earth.
Let us kneel with her and lovingly adore
Christ, her son, our God and King for evermore!

ANTHONY GREGORY MURRAY (1905–1992)

NOS GALAN

1 Deck the hall with boughs of hol-ly: *Fa la la la la, la la la la!*

'tis the sea-son to be jol-ly! *Fa la la la la, la la la la!*

Fill the mead cup, drain the bar-rel, *fa la la, fa la la, la la la!*____

v.3 to Coda

troll the an-cient Christ-mas ca-rol. *Fa la la la la, la la la la!*

Music: Welsh dance-carol, 18th century or earlier
        arranged by MALCOLM ARCHER (b. 1952)

2   See the flowing bowl before us!
    Strike the harp, and join the chorus!
    Follow me in merry measure,
    while I sing of beauty's treasure.

3   Fast away the old year passes,
    hail the new, ye lads and lasses!
    Laughing, quaffing, all together,
    Heedless of the wind and weather.

Welsh dance-carol from Edward Jones's
Musical and Poetical Relicks of the Welsh Bards, 1794

Ding- dong, ding, ___ ding - a - dong - a - ding. Ding- dong, ding- dong,

ding- a- dong, ding.   Up! good Christ-en folk, and list-en how the mer - ry
                       Tell the sto - ry, how from glo-ry God came down at

church_____ bells ring, and from stee-ple bid good peo - ple
Christ - - - - mas- tide, bring-ing glad- ness,_ chas-ing sad- ness,

come a - dore the new - - - born_ King. Born of mo - ther,
show'r-ing bless-ings far_____ and _ wide.

Music: Melody to *O quam mundum, quam jucundum*
   from *Piae Cantiones*, 1582
   harmonised by GEORGE RATCLIFFE WOODWARD (1848–1934)

CHRISTMAS

blest o'er o-ther,_ *Ex Ma - ri - a Vir - gi - ne,* in a sta-ble

('tis no fa-ble) *Chris-tus na-tus ho - - - di - e.*

The first four bars may be repeated at the end.

Ding-dong, ding, ding-a-dong-a-ding.
Ding-dong, ding-dong, ding-a-dong ding.

1   Up! good Christen folk, and listen
        how the merry church bells ring,
    and from steeple bid good people
        come adore the new-born King.

2   Tell the story, how from glory
        God came down at Christmastide,
    bringing gladness, chasing sadness,
        showering blessings far and wide.

3   Born of mother, blest o'er other,
        ex Maria Virgine,
    in a stable ('tis no fable)
        Christus natus hodie.

        [*Ding-dong, ding: ding-a-dong-a-ding.*
        Ding-dong, ding-dong, ding-a-dong ding.]

GEORGE RATCLIFFE WOODWARD (1848–1934)

The opening refrain may be repeated at the end.

1 Ding dong! mer-ri-ly on high   in heav'n the bells are ring - ing:
ding dong! ve-ri-ly the sky   is riv'n with an-gel sing - ing

Glo - - - - - - - -

- - - - ri - a, ho - san - na in ex - cel - sis!

Music: Melody of *Branle de l'Official* from
Thoinot Arbeau's dance manual *Orchésographie,* 1588
harmonised by CHARLES WOOD (1866–1926)

1   Ding dong! merrily on high
      in heaven the bells are ringing:
   ding dong! verily the sky
      is riven with angel singing
      Gloria, hosanna in excelsis!

2   E'en so here below, below,
      let steeple bells be swungen,
   and *i-o, i-o, i-o,*
      by priest and people sungen.
      Gloria, hosanna in excelsis!

3   Pray you, dutifully prime
      your matin chime, ye ringers;
   may you beautifully rhyme
      your eve-time song, ye singers:
      Gloria, hosanna in excelsis!

GEORGE RATCLIFFE WOODWARD (1848–1934)
in *Cambridge Carol Book,* 1924

EVERY STAR

1 Eve-ry star shall sing a ca-rol; eve-ry crea-ture, high or low, come and praise the King of Hea-ven, by what-ev-er name you know: *God a-bove, Man be-low, Ho-ly is the name I know.*

Music: SYDNEY CARTER (1915–2004)

1 Every star shall sing a carol;
    every creature, high or low,
  come and praise the King of Heaven,
    by whatever name you know:

    God above, Man below,
    holy is the name I know.

2 When the King of all creation
    had a cradle on the earth,
  holy was the human body,
    holy was the human birth:

3 Who can tell what other cradle
    high above the Milky Way
  still may rock the King of Heaven
    on another Christmas Day?

4 Who can count how many crosses
    still to come or long ago
  crucify the King of Heaven?
    Holy is the name I know:

5 Who can tell what other body
    he will hallow for his own?
  I will praise the Son of Mary,
    brother of my blood and bone:

6 Every star and every planet,
    every creature high and low
  come and praise the King of Heaven,
    by whatever name you know:

SYDNEY CARTER (1915–2004)

36 Words and Music: © 1961, Stainer & Bell Ltd, London, England <www.stainer.co.uk> Used by permission.

Music: Piae Cantiones, 1582

* If using the optional descant, the tenors may omit their part in the last line and double the bass part, or sing the melody an octave below so that all the sopranos can sing the descant.

15th century text, possibly Czech,
in *Piae Cantiones,* 1582

Light and nimble ♩=118

p lightly *mf* *p*

p Girls and boys, leave your toys, make no noise,
mp On that day far a-way Je-sus lay,
f Shep-herds came at the fame of thy name,

kneel at his crib and wor-ship him. At thy shrine, child di-vine,
an-gels were watch-ing round his head. Ho-ly child, Mo-ther mild,
an-gels their guide to Beth-le-hem. In that place, saw thy face

crib
watch - - - - ing
guide

Ah

Music: Czech folk tune
arranged by OLIVER TARNEY (*b.* 1984)

we are thine, our Sa-viour's here. ___
un - de - filed, we sing thy praise. ___
filled with grace, stood at thy door. ___

'Hal-le-lu-jah' the church bells ring,

If the *verse* is left accompanied, the *refrain* may be left unaccompanied from here.

'Hal-le-lu-jah' the An - gels sing, 'Hal-le-lu-jah' from ev - ery-thing.

All must draw near.
Our hearts we raise.
Love ev - er - more.

mf

1.2.

3. **Senza rall.**

1st time dim
2nd time cresc.

mp

pp

HAROLD MALCOLM WATTS SARGENT (1895–1967)

1 Girls and boys, leave your toys, make no noise,
  kneel at his crib and worship him.
At thy shrine, child divine, we are thine,
  our Saviour's here.

  'Hallelujah!' the church bells ring,
  'Hallelujah!' the angels sing,
  'Hallelujah!' from ev'rything.
    All must draw near.

2 On that day far away Jesus lay,
  angels were watching round his head,
Holy child, mother mild undefiled,
  we sing thy praise.
  'Hallelujah!' …
    Our hearts we raise.

3 Shepherds came at the fame of thy name,
  angels their guide to Bethlehem.
In that place saw thy face filled with grace,
  stood at thy door.
  'Hallelujah!' …
    Love evermore.

4 Wise men, too, haste to do homage new,
  gold, myrrh and frankincense they bring.
As 'twas said, starlight led to thy bed,
  bending their knee.
  'Hallelujah!' …
    Worshipping thee.

5 Oh, that we all might be good as he,
  spotless with God in unity.
Saviour dear, ever near with us here
  since life began.
  'Hallelujah!' …
    Godhead made man.

HAROLD MALCOLM WATTS SARGENT (1895–1967)

Although the musical setting uses the text of the first three verses only, the words
of the carol incorporating several further stanzas are presented here for information.

GOD REST YOU MERRY   Irregular

Music: English traditional melody
arranged by JOHN STAINER (1840–1901)
from *Christmas Carols New and Old* 1871
last verse arrangement by CHRISTOPHER ROBINSON (b. 1936)

1   God rest you merry, gentlemen,
      let nothing you dismay!
for Jesus Christ our Saviour
      was born on Christmas Day,
to save us all from Satan's power
      when we had gone astray:

        O tidings of comfort and joy,
          comfort and joy;
        O tidings of comfort and joy!

2   From God our heavenly Father
      a holy angel came;
the shepherds saw the glory
      and heard the voice proclaim
that Christ was born in Bethlehem —
      and Jesus is his name:

* 3   'Fear not,' then said the angel,
      'let nothing cause you fright;
to you is born a Saviour
      in David's town tonight,
to free all those who trust in him
      from Satan's power and might:'

4   The shepherds at these tidings
      rejoiced in heart and mind,
and on the darkened hillside
      they left their flocks behind,
and went to Bethlehem straightway
      this holy Child to find:

5   And when to Bethlehem they came,
      where Christ the infant lay,
they found him in a manger
      where oxen fed on hay;
and there beside her new-born child
      his mother knelt to pray:

Turn for arrangement of v. 6 with descant.

Descant / Unison

6 Now to the Lord sing prais - es, all peo-ple in this place;

6 Now to the Lord sing prais - es, all peo-ple in this place;

with Christ-ian love and fel - low-ship each o - ther now em - brace,

with Christ-ian love and fel - low-ship each o - ther now em - brace,

and let this Christ-mas fest - i - val all bit - ter-ness dis - place:

and let this Christ-mas fest - i - val all bit - ter-ness dis - place:

CHRISTMAS

IN DULCI JUBILO

Music: Later form of 14th-century German melody
adapted by JOHN STAINER (1840–1901)
based on arrangement by ROBERT LUCAS DE PEARSALL (1795–1856)

1   Good Christians all, rejoice
        with heart and soul and voice!
    Listen now to what we say,
        Jesus Christ is born today;
    ox and ass before him bow,
        and he is in the manger now!
            Christ is born today;
            Christ is born today!

2   Good Christians all, rejoice
        with heart and soul and voice!
    Hear the news of endless bliss,
        Jesus Christ was born for this:
    he has opened heaven's door,
        and we are blessed for evermore!
            Christ was born for this;
            Christ was born for this!

3   Good Christians all, rejoice
        with heart and soul and voice!
    Now you need not fear the grave;
        Jesus Christ was born to save:
    come at his most gracious call
        to find salvation, one and all!
            Christ was born to save;
            Christ was born to save!

In dulci jubilo
Latin and German, 14th century
adapted by JOHN MASON NEALE (1818–1866)*

TEMPUS ADEST FLORIDUM   76 76 D

Descant (*v. 5*)

In his mas-ter's steps he _ trod, where the snow lay dint - ed;

heat was in the ve - ry _ sod which the saint had _ print - ed.

There -fore, Chris -tian men, be sure, wealth or rank pos - sess - ing,

ye who now will bless the poor shall your-selves find bless - - ing.

Music: Melody to *Tempus adest floridum* in *Piae Cantiones,* 1582
arranged by JOHN STAINER (1840–1901)
Descant by MALCOLM ARCHER (*b.* 1952)

1   Good King Wenceslas look'd out
     on the Feast of Stephen,
 when the snow lay round about,
     deep and crisp and even;
 brightly shone the moon that night,
     though the frost was cruel,
 when a poor man came in sight,
     gath'ring winter fuel.

2   'Hither, page, and stand by me;
     if thou know'st it, telling —
 yonder peasant, who is he?
     where and what his dwelling?'
 'Sire, he lives a good league hence,
     underneath the mountain,
 right against the forest fence,
     by Saint Agnes' fountain.'

3   'Bring me flesh, and bring me wine!
     Bring me pine-logs hither!
 Thou and I will see him dine
     when we bear them thither.'
 Page and monarch forth they went,
     forth they went together;
 through the rude wind's wild lament
     and the bitter weather.

4 'Sire, the night is darker now,
   and the wind blows stronger;
fails my heart, I know now how,
   I can go no longer.'
'Mark my footsteps, good my page;
   tread thou in them boldly;
thou shalt find the winter's rage
   freeze thy blood less coldly.'

5 In his master's steps he trod,
   where the snow lay dinted;
heat was in the very sod
   which the saint had printed.
Therefore, Christian men, be sure,
   wealth or rank possessing,
ye who now will bless the poor
   shall yourselves find blessing.

JOHN MASON NEALE (1818–1866)

Thoughtfully (♩=60)

1 Good peo-ple all, this Christ-mas - time, con-si-der well, and bear in mind what our good God for us has done, in send-ing his be-lo-véd Son. With Ma-ry ho - ly we should pray to God with love, this Christ-mas

Music: Irishcarol, 19th century
arranged by OLIVER TARNEY (b. 1984)

The night before that happy tide,
the noble Virgin and her guide
were long-time seeking up and down
to find a lodging in the town.
But mark right well what came to pass
from every door repelled, alas.
As was foretold, their refuge all
was but a humble ox's stall.

Near Bethlehem did shepherds keep
their flocks of lambs and feeding sheep,
to whom God's angel did appear,
which put the shepherds in great fear.
'Arise and go,' the angels said,
'to Bethlehem. Be not afraid:
for there you'll find, this happy morn,
a princely babe, sweet Jesus, born.'

4 With thankful heart and joyful mind
the shepherds went the babe to find,
and, as God's angel had foretold,
they did our Saviour Christ behold.
Within a manger he was laid,
and by his side a virgin maid
attending on the Lord of Life,
who came on earth to end all strife.

5 There were three wise men from afar
directed by a glorious star,
and on they wandered, night and day,
until they came where Jesus lay;
and when they came unto that place,
where our beloved Messiah lay,
they humbly cast them at his feet,
with gifts of gold and incense sweet.

19th-century Irish carol from County Wexford,
and English words of a parallel tradition.

MENDELSSOHN

77 77 77 77 and refrain

Music: From a chorus by FELIX MENDELSSOHN-BARTHOLDY (1809–1847)
descant by DAVID WILLCOCKS (1919–2015)

1 Hark! the herald angels sing
   glory to the new-born King,
peace on earth and mercy mild,
   God and sinners reconciled.
Joyful, all ye nations rise,
   join the triumph of the skies;
with the angelic host proclaim,
   'Christ is born in Bethlehem.'

    Hark! the herald angels sing
    glory to the new-born King.

2 Christ, by highest heaven adored,
   Christ, the everlasting Lord,
late in time behold him come,
   offspring of a Virgin's womb!
Veiled in flesh the Godhead see:
   Hail, the incarnate Deity,
pleased as man with man to dwell,
   Jesus, our Emmanuel.

3 Hail, the heaven-born Prince of Peace!
   Hail, the Sun of Righteousness!
Light and life to all he brings,
   risen with healing in his wings.
Mild he lays his glory by,
   born that man no more may die,
born to raise the sons of earth,
   born to give them second birth.

           CHARLES WESLEY (1707–1788)
                and others

           Turn for arrangement of v.3 with descant.

3 Hail, the heaven-born Prince of Peace! Hail, the Sun of Right-eous-ness!

Light and life to all — he brings, risen with heal-ing — in his wings.

Mild he lays his — glo-ry by, — born that man no — more may die, —

born to raise the sons of earth, Born to give them se-cond birth.

ff

Hark! the he-rald an-gels sing glo-ry to the new-born King.

WIE SCHÖN LEUCHTET

887 887 48 48

Music: Melody by PHILIPP NICOLAI (1556–1608)
Harmony chiefly by JOHANN SEBASTIAN BACH (1685–1750)

1   How brightly shines the Morning Star!
The nations see and hail afar
   the light in Judah shining.
Thou David's son of Jacob's race,
the Bridegroom, and the King of grace,
   for thee our hearts are pining!
      Lowly, holy,
great and glorious, thou victorious
      Prince of graces,
filling all the heavenly places!

2   Though circled by the hosts on high,
he deigns to cast a pitying eye
   upon his helpless creature;
the whole creation's Head and Lord,
by highest seraphim adored,
   assumes our very nature.
      Jesus, grant us,
through thy merit, to inherit
      thy salvation;
hear, O hear our supplication.

3   Rejoice, ye heav'ns; thou Earth, reply;
with praise, ye sinners, fill the sky,
   for this his Incarnation.
Incarnate God, put forth thy power,
ride on, ride on, great Conqueror,
   till all know thy salvation.
      Amen, Amen!
Alleluia, Alleluia!
      Praise be given
evermore by earth and heaven.

German, PHILIPP NICOLAI (1556–1608)
v.1 HENRY HARBAUGH (1817–1867)*
and WILLIAM MERCER (1811–1873)

Music: MALCOLM ARCHER (*b.* 1952)

1   Hush! my dear, lie still and slumber;
        holy angels guard thy bed!
    Heav'nly blessings without number
        gently falling on thy head.

        Lullaby, lullaby,
            hush, my baby, lullaby.

2   Sleep, my babe; thy food and raiment,
        house and home thy friends provide:
    all without thy care or payment,
        all thy wants are well supplied.

3   Soft and easy is thy cradle,
        coarse and hard thy Saviour lay
    when his birth-place was a stable,
        and his softest bed was hay.

4   See the lovely babe addressing:
        lovely infant, how he smiled!
    When he wept, the mother's blessing
        soothed and hushed the holy child.

ISAAC WATTS (1674–1748)*
from *Moral Songs,* 1706

LONDONDERRY AIR   11 10 11 10 11 10 11 12

Music: Air from County Derry from *Irish Music as noted by George Petrie,* 1903
harmonised by JOHN BARNARD (*b.* 1948)

1   I cannot tell why he, whom angels worship,
       should set his love upon the sons of men,
or why, as Shepherd, he should seek the wanderers,
       to bring them back, they know not how or when.
But this I know, that he was born of Mary
       when Bethl'em's manger was his only home,
and that he lived at Nazareth and laboured,
and so the Saviour, Saviour of the world, is come.

2   I cannot tell how silently he suffered,
       as with his peace he graced this place of tears,
or how his heart upon the cross was broken,
       the crown of pain to three and thirty years.
But this I know, he heals the broken-hearted
       and stays our sin and calms our lurking fear
and lifts the burden from the heavy laden;
for still the Saviour, Saviour of the world is here.

3   I cannot tell how he will win the nations,
       how he will claim his earthly heritage,
how satisfy the needs and aspirations
       of east and west, of sinner and of sage.
But this I know, all flesh shall see his glory,
       and he shall reap the harvest he has sown,
and some glad day his sun will shine in splendour
when he the Saviour, Saviour of the world, is known.

4   I cannot tell how all the lands shall worship,
       when at his bidding every storm is stilled,
or who can say how great the jubilation
       when every heart with love and joy is filled.
But this I know, the skies will thrill with rapture,
       and myriad myriad human voices sing,
and earth to heav'n, and heav'n to earth, will answer,
'at last the Saviour, Saviour of the world, is King!'

WILLIAM YOUNG FULLERTON (1857–1932)

1 I   saw a   maid - en   sit - ten and sing: she
2 This ve - ry Lord, he   made all___ things,   and
3 There was sweet mu - sic at   this child's birth,   and
4 Heaven's an - gels sang to wel - come the child   now
5 Pray we   and sing on   this fes - tal day   that

lulled_ her_ child, a   lit - tle lord - - ing.
this___ ve - ry God, the King of all   kings.
heaven filled with an - - gels mak - ing much mirth.
born_ of a maid, all   un - - de - - filed.
peace_ may_ dwell with us___ al - - way.

Lul - lay, _____ lul - lay, _____ my   dear son, my sweet- ing. Lul-

- lay, ___ lul - lay, ___ my_ dear son, my_ own dear dear - - ing!

Music: Basque verse melody
        Refrain and arrangement of verse
        by CHARLES EDGAR PETTMAN (1866–1943)

1   I saw a maiden sitten and sing:
     she lulled her child, a little lording.

      Lullay, lullay, my dear son, my sweeting;
      lullay, lullay, my dear son, my own dear dearing.

2   This very Lord, he made all things,
     and this very God, the King of all kings.

3   There was sweet music at this child's birth,
     and heaven filled with angels making much mirth.

4   Heaven's angels sang to welcome the child
     now born of a maid, all undefiled.

5   Pray we and sing on this festal day
     that peace may dwell with us alway.

British Library, Sloane MS 2593, modernised
15th century or earlier

Music: Melody as given in *Christmas Carols New and Old,* 1871
harmonised by GERALD HOCKEN KNIGHT (1908–1979)
Descant by CRAIG SELLAR LANG (1891–1971)

1   I saw three ships come sailing in
      on Christmas Day, on Christmas Day.
    I saw three ships come sailing in
      on Christmas Day in the morning.

2   And what was in those ships all three?
    And what was in those ships all three?

3   Our Saviour Christ and his lady,
    Our Saviour Christ and his lady

4   Pray whither sailed those ships all three?
    Pray whither sailed those ships all three?

5   Oh, they sailed into Bethlehem,
    Oh, they sailed into Bethlehem

6   And all the bells on earth shall ring,
    And all the bells on earth shall ring

7   And all the Angels in Heaven shall sing,
    And all the Angels in Heaven shall sing

8   And all the souls on earth shall sing,
    And all the souls on earth shall sing

9   Then let us all rejoice, amain,
    Then let us all rejoice, amain!

English carol possibly derived from
German folk song, 17th century or earlier

Music: LENNOX BERKELEY (1903–1989)

1   I sing of a maiden
      that is makeless;
   King of all kinges,
      to her son she ches.

2   He came all so stille
      where his mother was,
   as dew in Aprile
      that falleth on the grass.

3   He came all so stille
      to his mother's bower,
   as dew in Aprile
      that falleth on the flower.

4   He came all so stille
      where his mother lay,
   as dew in Aprile
      that falleth on the spray.

5   Mother and maiden
      was never none but she;
   well may such a lady
      Godès mother be.

British Library, Sloane MS 2593, modernised
15th century or earlier

Music: Melody based on an Appalachian folk carol fragment
JOHN JACOB NILES (1892–1980)
arranged by ANDREW CARTER (b. 1939)

CHRISTMAS

you and like I ... I won-der as I wan-der out un-der the sky.

2 When Ma-ry birthed Je-sus 'twas in a cow's stall, with

2 When Ma-ry birthed Je-sus 'twas in a cow's stall, with

2 When Ma-ry birthed Je-sus 'twas in a cow's stall, with

2 When Ma-ry birthed Je-sus 'twas in a cow's stall, with

CHRISTMAS

CHRISTMAS

you and like I ... I won-der as I wan-der out

under the sky.

Mm

Mm

Mm

1   I wonder as I wander out under the sky,
       how Jesus the Saviour did come for to die.
    For poor on'ry people like you and like I …
       I wonder as I wander out under the sky.

2   When Mary birthed Jesus 'twas in a cow's stall,
       with wise men and farmers and shepherds and all.
    But high from God's heaven a star's light did fall,
       and the promise of ages it then did recall.

3   If Jesus had wanted for any wee thing,
       a star in the sky, or a bird on the wing,
    or all of God's angels in heav'n for to sing,
       he surely could have it, 'cause he was the King.

JOHN JACOB NILES (1892–1980)
based on an Appalachian folk carol fragment,
collected 1933

CRANHAM   Irregular

1 In the bleak mid - win - ter fro - sty wind made
2 Our God, heaven can - not hold _ him nor _ earth sus -
3 E - nough for him, whom che - ru - bim wor - ship night and
4 An - gels and arch - an - - gels may have ga - thered
5 What _ can I give _ him, poor _ as I

moan, earth stood hard as i - - - ron,
- tain; heaven and earth shall flee a - way
day, a breast - - ful of milk _ and a
there, che - ru - bim and se - ra - phim
am? If I were a shep - - herd

wa - ter like a stone; snow had fal - len,
when he comes to reign: in the bleak mid -
man - ger - ful of hay; e - nough for him, whom
thronged _ the air; but on - - ly his
I would bring a lamb, if I were a

Music: GUSTAV HOLST (1874–1934)

CHRISTMAS

snow on snow, snow___ on___ snow,
-win - - ter a sta - ble - place suf - ficed the
an - - gels fall___ down be - fore, the
mo - - ther in her maid - en bliss
wise___ man I would do my part, — yet

in the bleak mid - win - ter long___ a - - go.
Lord___ God Al - migh - ty Je - - sus___ Christ.
ox and ass and ca - mel which a - - dore.
wor - shipped the Be - lov - èd with___ a___ kiss.
what I can I give him, give___ my___ heart.

CHRISTINA GEORGINA ROSSETTI (1830–1894)

Music: Polish traditional carol
arranged by DAVID WILLCOCKS (1919–2015)

CHRISTMAS

CAROLS ANCIENT & MODERN

1   Infant holy, Infant lowly,
        for his bed a cattle stall;
     oxen lowing, little knowing
        Christ the Babe is Lord of all.
     Swift are winging angels singing,
        Nowells ringing, tidings bringing:
     Christ the Babe is Lord of all,
     Christ the Babe is Lord of all.

2   Flocks were sleeping, shepherds keeping ⌣
        vigil till the morning new;
     saw the glory, heard the story,
        tidings of a gospel true.
     Thus rejoicing, free from sorrow,
        praises voicing, greet the morrow:
     Christ the Babe was born for you!
     Christ the Babe was born for you!

                    Polish carol *W zlobie lezy*
            translated 1921 by EDITH REED

NOEL

DCM

Music: English traditional melody
adapted *by* ARTHUR SEYMOUR SULLIVAN (1842–1900)
descant by DAVID WILLCOCKS (1919–2015)

1   It came upon the midnight clear,
     that glorious song of old,
  from angels bending near the earth
     to touch their harps of gold:
  'Peace on the earth, good will to men,
     from heaven's all-gracious King!'
  the world in solemn stillness lay
     to hear the angels sing.

2   Still through the cloven skies they come,
     with peaceful wings unfurled;
  and still their heavenly music floats
     o'er all the weary world:
  above its sad and lowly plains
     they bend on hovering wing;
  and ever o'er its Babel-sounds
     the blessèd angels sing.

3   Yet with the woes of sin and strife
     the world has suffered long;
  beneath the angel strain have rolled
     two thousand years of wrong;
  and man, at war with man, hears not
     the love-song which they bring:
  O hush the noise, ye men of strife,
     and hear the angels sing.

4   For lo, the days are hastening on,
     by prophet-bards foretold,
  when, with the ever-circling years,
     comes round the age of gold;
  when peace shall over all the earth
     its ancient splendours fling,
  and the whole world give back the song
     which now the angels sing.

EDMUND HAMILTON SEARS (1810–1876)

Turn for v.4 arrangement with descant.

CAROLS ANCIENT & MODERN

v.1 Unison
v.5 Round (optional, entries at circled numbers)

1 The tree of life my soul hath seen, la - den with fruit and
5 This fruit doth make my soul to thrive, it keeps my dy - ing

al - ways green: the tree of life my soul hath seen, la -
faith a - live; this fruit doth make my soul to thrive, it

-den with fruit and al - ways green: the trees of na - ture
keeps my dy - ing faith a - live; which makes my soul in

fruit - less be com - pared with Christ the ap - ple tree.
haste to be with Je - sus Christ the ap - ple tree.

SSAA unaccompanied (or S(S) accompanied)

2 His beau - ty doth all things ex - cel: by faith I know, but ne'er can tell; his

beau - ty doth all things ex - cel: by faith I know, but ne'er can tell the

Music: ELIZABETH POSTON (1905–1987)

CHRISTMAS

cresc.

glo - ry which I now can see in Je - sus Christ the ap - ple tree.

4 part, or Unison accompanied

3 For hap - pi - ness I long have sought, and plea - sure dear - ly
4 I'm wea - ry with my for - mer toil, here I will sit and

I have bought: for hap-pi-ness I long have sought, and plea-sure dear-ly
rest a - while: I'm wea-ry with my for - mer toil, here I will sit and

I have bought: I missed of all, but now I see 'tis
rest a - while: un - der the sha - dow I will be, of

Optional ending, last time
(accompaniment only)

found in Christ the ap - ple tree.
Je - sus Christ the ap - ple tree.

ANONYMOUS
From the collection of Joshua Smith,
New Hampshire, 1784

ANTIOCH (COMFORT (Mason))   CM extended

1 Joy to the world, the Lord is come! let earth re-ceive her King; let ev - - ery __ heart __ pre - pare __ him __ room, __ and heav'n and na - ture _ sing, and heav'n and na - ture sing. and heav'n and na-ture sing. and sing, and heav'n, and heav'n __ and na - ture sing.

heav'n and na-ture sing, and heav'n and na - ture sing.

Music: W. Holford's *Voce di Melodia*, *c.*1834
    arranged by LOWELL MASON (1792–1872)

1   Joy to the world, the Lord is come!
      let earth receive her King;
    let every heart prepare him room,
      and heaven and nature sing,
        and heaven and nature sing,
        and heaven, and heaven and nature sing.

2   Joy to the world, the Saviour reigns!
      let all their songs employ;
    while fields and floods, rocks, hills and plains
      repeat the sounding joy,
        repeat the sounding joy,
        repeat, repeat the sounding joy.

3   He rules the world with truth and grace,
      and makes the nations prove
    the glories of his righteousness
      and wonders of his love,
        and wonders of his love,
        and wonders, wonders of his love.

ISAAC WATTS (1674–1748)

1 King Je-sus hath a gar-den, full of di - vers flow'rs, where

I go cull-ing po-sies gay, all times and hours. *There naught is heard but*
(6) That I may hear this

Pa - ra - dise bird, harp, dul-ci-mer, lute, with cym - bal,
mu - sic clear:

trump and tym-bal, and the ten-der, sooth-ing flute; with cym - bal,

Music: Dutch carol melody, 17th century
harmonised by CHARLES WOOD (1866–1926)

trump and tym-bal, and the ten - der, sooth-ing flute.

2   The Lily, white in blossom there, is Chastity:
the Violet, with sweet perfume, Humility.

3   The bonny Damask-rose is known as Patïence:
the blithe and thrifty Marygold, Obedience.

4   The Crown Imperial bloometh too in yonder place,
'tis Charity, of stock divine, the flower of grace.

5   Yet, 'mid the brave, the bravest prize of all may claim ⌣
the Star of Bethlem – Jesus – blessèd be his Name!

6   Ah! Jesu Lord, my heal and weal, my bliss complete,
make thou my heart thy garden-plot, fair, trim and neat.
That I may hear this music clear:
harp, dulcimer, lute,
with cymbal, trump and tymbal,
and the tender, soothing flute;
with cymbal, trump and tymbal,
and the tender, soothing flute.

17th-century Dutch carol *Heer Jesus heeft een Hofken*
translated by GEORGE RATCLIFFE WOODWARD (1848–1934)

1 List-en to the mes-sage that the an-gels bring, tell-ing fright-ened shep-herds of a new-born King: 'Glo-ry to God in hea-ven, peace to the earth is gi-ven, Christ is born, Christ is born.' 2 List-en to the

Music: Moravian traditional melody
arranged by DAVID ILIFF (b. 1939)

CHRISTMAS

shep-herds as they shout for joy: 'Let us go to Beth-le-hem and

see this boy. He brings us all sal-va- tion– give him your a-dor-a- tion –

Christ is born! Christ is born!'

3 In the sta-ble won-d'ring shep-herds kneel in awe, gaz-ing at the

Christ is King, — Christ is — King!

Christ is King, Christ is King!

1 Listen to the message that the angels bring,
      telling frightened shepherds of a newborn King:
      'Glory to God in heaven,
      peace to the earth is given,
      Christ is born, Christ is born.'

2 Listen to the shepherds as they shout for joy:
      'Let us go to Bethlehem and see this boy.
      He brings us all salvation –
      give him your adoration –
      Christ is born! Christ is born!'

3 In the stable wondering shepherds kneel in awe,
      gazing at the holy baby in the straw,
      'Is this the one who's given?
      Yes, he's the King of heaven!
      Christ is born! Christ is born!'

4 Join the happy shepherds as they all rejoice,
      shout and sing and praise him with your heart and voice.
      Born of a humble mother,
      Jesus, our friend and brother,
      Christ is King, Christ is King!

DAVID ILIFF (*b.* 1939)

1 Lit - tle don - - key, lit-tle don - - key, on a du - - sty road, got to keep on plod-ding on - - ward with your pre - cious load:

2 Been a long time, lit-tle don - - key, through the win - - ter's night — don't give up now, lit - tle don - - key, Beth - le-hem's in sight.

Ring out those bells to - night, Beth - le - hem, Beth-le - hem; fol - - low that

Music: ERIC BOSWELL, (ERIC SIMPSON) (1921–2009)
arranged by NOËL TREDINNICK (b. 1949)

CHRISTMAS

star to - night, Beth - le - hem, Beth - le - hem! 3 Lit - tle don - key,

lit - tle don - key, had a hea - vy day — lit - tle don - key,

car - ry Ma - ry safe - ly on her way. way.

Coda *(optional)*

Lit - tle don - key, car - ry Ma - ry safe - ly on her way.

Lit - tle don - key, car - ry Ma - ry safe - ly on her way.

ERIC BOSWELL (1921–2009)

1 Lit - tle Je - sus, sweet-ly sleep, do not stir; we will lend a
2 Ma - ry's lit - tle ba - by, sleep, sweet-ly sleep, sleep in com - fort,

coat of fur. We will rock you, rock you, rock you.
slum - ber deep.

We will rock you, rock you, rock you. See the fur to
We will serve you

keep you warm, snug - ly round your ti - ny form.
all we can, dar - ling, dar - ling lit - tle man.

PERCY DEARMER (1867–1936)
Based on Czech carol *Hajej, nynjej, Jezisku*

Music: Czech cradle-rocking carol
harmonised by MARTIN SHAW (1875–1958)

LOVE CAME DOWN   67 67

1   Love came down at Christmas,
     love all lovely, Love divine;
  love was born at Christmas,
     star and angels gave the sign.

2   Worship we the Godhead,
     love incarnate, Love divine;
  worship we our Jesus:
     but wherewith for sacred sign?

3   Love shall be our token,
     love be yours and love be mine,
  Love to God and all men,
     love for plea and gift and sign.

CHRISTINA GEORGINA ROSSETTI (1830–1894)

Music: MALCOLM ARCHER (b. 1952)

Allegro moderato (♩ = 112)

v.1 f
v.2 mf

Verse   Soprano   *mf*

1 I saw a fair maid - en _ sit - ten and sing. She
2 That same Lord is he _ that made al - le thing; of

mf

v.2 cresc.

rall.

tenuti v.2 only

lul - led a lit - tle child, a swee - te lord - ing.
al - le lord - is he is lord, of al - le king - es King.

v.2 cresc.

Music: RICHARD RUNCIMAN TERRY (1865–1938)

CHRISTMAS

Turn for verses 3 & 4.

a tempo

mf

Soprano   *mf*

3 There was mick - le me-lo-dy at that child-es   birth:
4 An - gels bright sang their song to that child; 'Bless-

mf

cresc.

molto rall.
tenuti v.3 only

All   that were in heav'n-ly bliss, they   made   mick - le mirth.
-ed be thou, and so   be   she, so   meek and so   mild.'

cresc.

CHRISTMAS

British Library, Sloane MS 2593, modernised
15th century or earlier

COVENTRY CAROL   44 6 D and refrain

The Refrain is sung again after the third verse.

Music: English 15th-century melody (later form)
        arranged by MARTIN SHAW (1875–1958)

Lully, lulla,
thou little tiny child,
by by, lully lullay.

1   O sisters too,
     how may we do
for to preserve this day
     this poor youngling,
     for whom we do sing
by by, lully lullay?

2   Herod the king,
     in his raging,
chargèd he hath this day
     his men of might,
     in his own sight,
all young childrèn to slay.

3   That woe is me,
     poor child for thee!
and ever morn and day,
     for thy parting
     neither say nor sing
by by, lully lullay!

Lully, lulla,
thou little tiny child,
by by, lully lullay.

English, 15th century

The refrain is sung at the start and after verse 3 only.

Music: African American traditional carol
arranged by MALCOLM ARCHER (b. 1952)

yes, Lord! *Ah*

what did she name him?
where was he born?
where did she lay him?

The peo-ple keep a-com-ing but the

train has gone!

7 Laid him in a man-ger, yes, Lord,

laid him in a man-ger, yes, my Lord, laid him in a man-ger,

yes, Lord! *The peo-ple keep a-com-ing but the train has gone!*

African American traditional carol
collected in *St Helens Island Spirituals,* 1925 *

Music: Irish folk song
   arranged by CHARLES WOOD (1866–1926)

CHRISTMAS

1 Fair maid-en, who is this bairn that thou bear-est in thine arm? Sir, it is a king-es son that in heav'n a-bove doth wone. Ma-ter o-ra Fi-li-um

2 Man to fa-ther he hath none but him-self, God a-lone, of a maid he would be born to save man-kind that was for-lorn.

ut post hox ex - i - li - um,   no - bis do - net gau - di - um

be - a - to - rum   om - ni - um!

p

3 Three   kings brought him pre - sents,   gold, _ myrrh and frank - in - cense,

mp

CHRISTMAS

to my son ___ full of might, King of kings and Lord of right.

Ma - ter o - ra Fi - li - um ut post hoc ex - i - li - um,

no - bis do - net gau - di - um be - a - to - rum om - ni - um!

4 Fair maid-en, pray for us un-to thy Son, sweet Je-sus, that he will send us, of his grace, in heav'n on high to have a place. *Ma-ter o-ra Fi-li-um*

ut post hoc ex - i - li - um, no - bis do - net gau - di - um be - a - to - rum om - - ni - um!

Oxford, Balliol College MS 354 p.374,
English, 15th century *

Music: Cornish traditional melody, collected by the Revd G.H. Doble
arranged by MALCOLM ARCHER (b. 1952)

1   Now the holly bears a berry as white as the milk,
    and Mary bore Jesus, all wrapped up in silk:
        And Mary bore Jesus Christ our Saviour for to be,
            and the first tree in the greenwood, it was the holly,
                holly, holly!
        And the first tree in the greenwood, it was the holly!

2   Now the holly bears a berry as green as the grass,
    and Mary bore Jesus, who died on the cross:

3   Now the holly bears a berry as black as the coal,
    and Mary bore Jesus, who died for us all:

4   Now the holly bears a berry, as blood is it red,
    then trust we our Saviour, who rose from the dead:

vv.1-3, Cornish traditional carol,
collected by the Revd G.H. Doble
v.4 Editors of *The Oxford Book of Carols*, 1928
after a later Cornish version by W.D. Watson

ADESTE FIDELES   Irregular

Music: Melody probably by JOHN FRANCIS WADE (*c.*1711–1786)
harmonised by Compilers of *The English Hymnal,* 1906
vv. 6 & 7 arranged by DAVID WILLCOCKS (1919–2015)

1   O come, all ye faithful,
      joyful and triumphant,
O come ye, O come ye to Bethlehem;
    come and behold him
    born the King of Angels:
      O come, let us adore him,
      O come, let us adore him,
      O come, let us adore him,
        Christ the Lord!

2   God of God,
    Light of Light,
lo! he abhors not the Virgin's womb;
    very God,
    begotten, not created:

3   See how the shepherds,
    summoned to his cradle,
leaving their flocks, draw nigh with lowly fear;
    we too will thither
    bend our joyful footsteps:

* 4   Lo! star-led chieftains,
    Magi, Christ adoring,
offer him incense, gold, and myrrh;
    we to the Christ child
    bring our heart's oblations:

* 5   Child, for us sinners
    poor and in the manger,
fain we embrace thee, with awe and love;
    who would not love thee,
    loving us so dearly?

Turn for arrangement of v.6 with descant, and v.7.

CHRISTMAS

CAROLS ANCIENT & MODERN

Je--su, to thee be glo--ry giv'n;

Word of the Fa-ther, now in flesh ap-pear-ing: O

come, let us a-dore him, O come, let us a-dore him, O

come, let us a-dore him, Christ the Lord!

Adeste, fideles, (Latin, 18th century)
translated by FREDERICK OAKELEY (1802–1880) and others

Andante ♩. = 80

1 O ho - ly night! ___ the stars are bright - ly shin - - - - ing, it is the night of our dear Sav - iour's birth.

2 Drawn by the light ___ of faith se - rene - ly beam - - - ing, with glow - ing hearts by his cra - dle we stand.

Music: ADOLPHE ADAM (1803–1856)
     arranged by JOHN BARNARD (b. 1948)

Long lay the world ___ in sin and er - ror
Led by the star, ___ its light so sweet - ly

world in sin
star, its light

pin - - - - ing, till he ap-peared and the soul felt its
gleam - - - ing, here come the wise men from far dis - tant

CHRISTMAS

worth.
land.

A thrill of hope, the wea - ry world re-
The King of kings lay thus in low - ly

cresc.

-joi - ces, for yon - der breaks a new and glo-rious morn.
man - ger, in all our tri - als, born to be our friend.

cresc.

CHRISTMAS

1 O holy night! the stars are brightly shining,
    it is the night of our dear Saviour's birth.
Long lay the world in sin and error pining,
    till he appeared and the soul felt its worth.
A thrill of hope, the weary world rejoices,
    for yonder breaks a new and glorious morn.
Fall on your knees and hear the angel voices,
    O night divine, O night when Christ was born.

2 Drawn by the light of faith serenely beaming,
    with glowing hearts by his cradle we stand.
Led by the star, its light so sweetly gleaming,
    here come the wise men from far distant land.
The King of kings lay thus in lowly manger,
    in all our trials, born to be our friend.
He knows our need, and guards us all from danger;
    behold your King! Before the Christ child bend.

Minuit, chrétiens by
PLACIDE CAPPEAU (1808–1877)
translated by JOHN SULLIVAN DWIGHT (1812–1893)

QUITTEZ PASTEURS

Music: Besançon carol melody
       arranged by DAVID ILIFF (*b.* 1939)

1   O leave your sheep, you shepherds on the hillside,
leave all your sheep, and greet your newborn King;
for Christ is born, your sorrow can become your joy,
    your God is Saviour too —
     Go now! Go now!
    The Christ is born in Bethlehem!
     Go now! Go now!
    The Christ is born in Bethlehem!

2   You'll find him there, this tiny little baby,
his cradle bed where cattle feed on hay!
He lies asleep; he loves you with unheard of love,
    your God is shepherd too —
     Go now! Go now!
    Your faithful shepherd cares for you!
     Go now! Go now!
    Your faithful shepherd cares for you!

3   A boy is King! You eastern men of wisdom,
pursue the light that leads you to the Sun,
the rising Sun. This child is God incarnate,
    he is God your Sovereign, too —
     Bow down! Bow down!
    Present your incense, gold and myrrh!
     Bow down! Bow down!
    Present your incense, gold and myrrh!

4   We pray you now, God's one and Holy Spirit,
to pierce our hearts with your eternal love,
give us your peace. For God will bring us heaven
    through our faith in Christ the Lord —
     Come now! Come now!
    Come now and fill our hearts with love!
     Come now! Come now!
    Come now and fill our hearts with love!

French traditional carol *Quittez, pasteurs, vos brebis,*
18th century or earlier
translated by BILL STEAD, (PAUL WIGMORE) (1925–2014)

Music: German chorale melody first in Scheidt's *Tabulatur-Buch,* 1650
harmonised by JOHANN SEBASTIAN BACH (1685–1750)

1   O little one sweet, O little one mild,
     thy Father's purpose thou hast fulfilled;
         thou cam'st from heaven to mortal ken,
         equal to be with us poor men,
     O little one sweet, O little one mild.

2   O little one sweet, O little one mild,
     with joy thou hast the whole world filled;
         thou camest here from heaven's domain,
         to bring men comfort in their pain,
     O little one sweet, O little one mild.

3   O little one sweet, O little one mild,
     in thee Love's beauties are all distilled;
         then light in us thy love's bright flame,
         that we may give thee back the same,
     O little one sweet, O little one mild.

4   O little one sweet, O little one mild,
     help us to do as thou hast willed.
         Lo, all we have belongs to thee!
         Ah, keep us in our fealty!
     O little one sweet, O little one mild.

German late-mediaeval carol *O Jesulein süss*
translated by Editors of *The Oxford Book of Carols,* 1928

FOREST GREEN   DCM

1 O little town of Bethlehem,
   how still we see thee lie!
above thy deep and dreamless sleep
   the silent stars go by:
yet in thy dark streets shineth
   the everlasting Light;
the hopes and fears of all the years
   are met in thee tonight.

2 O morning stars, together
   proclaim the holy birth,
and praises sing to God the King,
   and peace to men on earth.
For Christ is born of Mary;
   and, gathered all above,
while mortals sleep, the angels keep
   their watch of wondering love.

3 How silently, how silently,
   the wondrous gift is given!
so God imparts to human hearts
   the blessings of his heaven.
No ear may hear his coming;
   but in this world of sin,
where meek souls will receive him, still
   the dear Christ enters in.

CHRISTMAS

Descant (v. 4)

4 O ho - ly Child of Beth - le - hem, de - scend to us, we pray;

Unison

cast out our sin, and en - ter in: be born in us to - day.

We hear the Christ-mas an - - gels the great glad tid - ings tell:

O come to us, a - bide with us, our Lord Em-ma-nu - el.

PHILLIPS BROOKS (1835–1893)

Music: English traditional melody
harmonised by RALPH VAUGHAN WILLIAMS (1872–1958)
last verse arrangement by THOMAS ARMSTRONG (1898–1994)

white an - - - - - gel

We shep - herds poor_____

Lul - la - by,

Lul - - - - la -
Lul - - la,

Lul - la -

Music: CARL BORROMÄUS NEUNER (1778–1830) and others
from the arrangement by CHARLES MACPHERSON (1870–1927)

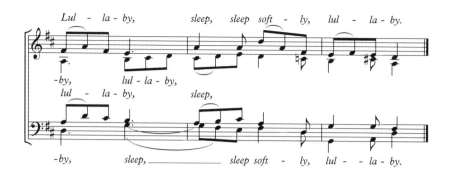

1   O sleep thou heaven-born treasure thou,
         sleep sound, thou dearest child;
     white angel wings shall fan thy brow
         with breezes soft and mild.
     We shepherds poor are here to sing
         a simple lullay to our king.
             Lullaby, lullaby,
             sleep, sleep softly,
             lullaby.

2   See Mary has with mother's love
         a bed for thee outspread,
     while Joseph stoops him from above,
         and watches at thy head.
     The lambkins in the stall so nigh,
         that thou mayest sleep, have hushed their cry.

3   On mother's knee doth man repose
         while he a child remains:
     but when the child to manhood grows,
         then knows he woes and pains.
     O holy Child, give grace to all,
         that we endure whate'er befall.

German carol *Schlaf wohl, du Himmelsknabe du*
CHRISTIAN FRIEDRICH DANIEL SCHUBART (1739–1791) and others
vv.1,2 ARTHUR FOXTON FERGUSON (1866–1920)
and Editors of *The New Oxford Book of Carols*, 1992

DIVINUM MYSTERIUM   87 87 87 7

1   Of the Father's heart begotten
          ere the world from chaos rose,
       he is Alpha: from that Fountain,
          all that is and hath been flows;
       he is Omega, of all things
          yet to come the mystic Close,
             evermore and evermore.

Music: Melody from *Piæ Cantiones*, 1582
        harmonised by Compilers of *New English Hymnal*, 1986

2   By his word was all created;
      he commanded and 'twas done;
    earth and sky and boundless ocean,
      universe of three in one,
    all that sees the moon's soft radiance,
      all that breathes beneath the sun,
        evermore and evermore.

3   He assumed this mortal body,
      frail and feeble, doomed to die,
    that the race from dust created
      might not perish utterly,
    which the dreadful Law had sentenced
      in the depths of hell to lie,
        evermore and evermore.

4   O how blest that wondrous birthday,
      when the Maid the curse retrieved,
    brought to birth mankind's salvation,
      by the Holy Ghost conceived,
    and the Babe, the world's Redeemer,
      in her loving arms received,
        evermore and evermore.

5   This is he, whom seer and sybil
      sang in ages long gone by;
    this is he of old revealèd
      in the page of prophecy;
    lo! he comes, the promised Saviour;
      let the world his praises cry!
        evermore and evermore.

6   Sing, ye heights of heaven, his praises;
      Angels and Archangels, sing!
    wheresoe'er ye be, ye faithful,
      let your joyous anthems ring,
    every tongue his name confessing,
      countless voices answering,
        evermore and evermore.

Corde natus ex parentis
AURELIUS CLEMENS PRUDENTIUS (348–*c.*413)
translated by ROBY FURLEY DAVIS (1866–1937)

1 On Christ-mas night_ all Chris-tians sing to hear the news_ the

an - gels bring; on Christ-mas night_ all Chris-tians sing_ to

hear the news the an - gels bring:_ news of great joy,_ news of_ great

mirth,_ news of_ our_ mer-ci-ful King's birth._

Fine

Music: English traditional Sussex melody
arranged by MALCOLM ARCHER (*b.* 1952)

CHRISTMAS

before v.2

before v.3

2   Then why should men on earth be so sad,
       since our Redeemer made us glad,
    when from our sin he set us free,
       all for to gain our liberty?

3   All out of darkness we have light,
       which made the angels sing this night:
    'Glory to God and peace to men,
       now and for evermore, Amen!'

English traditional carol
based on a carol by LUKE WADDING (1588–1657)

IRBY

87 87 77

Music: Melody by HENRY JOHN GAUNTLETT (1805–1876)
harmonised by ARTHUR HENRY MANN (1850–1929)
last verse arrangement by DAVID WILLCOCKS (1919–2015)

1 Once in royal David's city
    stood a lowly cattle shed,
where a mother laid her baby
    in a manger for his bed:
Mary was that mother mild,
Jesus Christ her little child.

2 He came down to earth from heaven
    who is God and Lord of all,
and his shelter was a stable,
    and his cradle was a stall;
with the poor and mean and lowly
lived on earth our Saviour holy.

* 3 And through all his wondrous childhood
    he would honour and obey,
love and watch the lowly maiden,
    in whose gentle arms he lay:
Christian children all must be
mild, obedient, good as he.

* 4 For he is our childhood's pattern,
    day by day like us he grew,
he was little, weak, and helpless,
    tears and smiles like us he knew;
and he feeleth for our sadness,
and he shareth in our gladness.

5 And our eyes at last shall see him,
    through his own redeeming love,
for that child so dear and gentle
    is our Lord in heaven above;
and he leads his children on
to the place where he is gone.

Turn for last verse arrangement with descant.

CECIL FRANCES ALEXANDER (1818–1895)

Refrain

Past three o'-clock, and a cold fros-ty morn - ing. Past three o' - clock; good

Last time *Fine* *Verse*

mor-row mas-ters all! 1 Born is a ba - by, gen - tle as

may be, Son of__ th'e - ter - nal Fa - ther su - per-nal.

D.C.

Music: Tune *London Waits* from *Apollo's Banquet* 1663
harmonised by CHARLES WOOD (1866–1926)

2   Seraph quire singeth,
    angel bell ringeth;
    hark how they rime it,
    time it and chime it.

3   Mid earth rejoices
    hearing such voices
    ne'ertofore so well
    carolling *Nowell*.

4   Hinds o'er the pearly,
    dewy lawn early
    seek the high stranger
    laid in the manger.

5   Cheese from the dairy
    bring they for Mary,
    and, not for money,
    butter and honey.

6   Light out of star-land
    leadeth from far land
    princes, to meet him,
    worship and greet him.

7   Myrrh from full coffer,
    incense they offer;
    nor is the golden
    nugget withholden.

8   Thus they: I pray you,
    up, sirs, nor stay you
    till ye confess him
    likewise and bless him.

GEORGE RATCLIFFE WOODWARD (1848–1934)
based on a call of the London Waits

Music: Dorset church-gallery tune-book
  arranged by THOMAS REGINALD JACQUES (1894–1969)

1 Rejoice and be merry
 in songs and in mirth!
O praise our Redeemer;
 all mortals on earth!
For this is the birthday
 of Jesus our King,
who brought us salvation,
 his praises we'll sing!

2 A heavenly vision
 appeared in the sky;
vast numbers of angels
 the shepherds did spy,
proclaiming the birthday of
 Jesus our King,
who brought us salvation,
 his praises we'll sing!

3 Likewise a bright star
 in the sky did appear,
which led the wise men
 from the East to draw near;
they found the Messiah,
 sweet Jesus our King,
who brought us salvation,
 his praises we'll sing!

4 And when they were come,
 they their treasures unfold,
and unto him offered
 myrrh, incense and gold.
So blessèd for ever
 be Jesus our King,
who brought us salvation,
 his praises we'll sing!

Dorset church-gallery tune-book, 19th
century or earlier

Music: attributed to Mateo Flecha, the elder (1481–1553)

    edited by Grayston Ives (b. 1948)

CHRISTMAS

1 El lo - bo ra - bio - so la____ qui - so mor -
2 Es - te qu'es na - ci - do es____ el gran mo -
3 Mu - chas pro - fe - ci - as lo han____ pro - fe - ti -
4 Yo vi mil gar - zo - nes que an - - da - van can -
5 Es - te vie - ne a dar____ a____ los muer - tos
6 Pues que ya te - ne - mos lo____ que des - se -

- der,____ mas Dios Po - de - ro - so la su - po de - fen -
-nar - ca, Chris - to pa - tri - ar - ca de____ car - ne ves -
-za - do; y aun en nues-tros di - as lo he - mos al can -
-tan - do, por a - qui vo - lan - do ha - - cien-do mil
vi - da, y vie - ne a re - par - ar de to - - dos la ca -
- a - mos, to - dos jun - tos va - mos, pre - - sen - tes lle -

-der; qui - so la ha - cer que no
-ti - - do; ha - nos re - di - mi - - do con
-za - - do. a Dios hu - ma - na - - do ve -
so - - nes, di - zien - do a gas - co - - nes: 'Glo -
-i - - da; es la Luz del Di - - a a -
-ve - - mos; to - dos le da - re - - mos nues-

pu - die - se pe - car, ni aun o - ri - gi -
se ha - zer chi - qui - to: aun - que' - era in - fi -
- mos en el sue - - lo, y al hom - bre nel
- - ria sea en el cie - - lo, y paz en el
- - que - ste mo - zue - - lo; es - te es el cor -
- - tra vo - lun - tad, pues a se i - gua -

-nal es - ta Vir - gen no tu vie - - ra.
-ni - - to, fi - ni - to se hi - zie - - ra.
cie - - lo por - - - qu'el lo qui - sie - - ra.
sue - - lo, qu'es____ Je - sus nas - cie - - ra.'
-de - - ro que San Juan di - xe - - ra.
-lar con el____ hom - bre vi - nie - - ra.

attributed to MATEO FLECHA, THE ELDER (1481–1553)

HUMILITY (OXFORD)   77 77 and refrain

Unison

Refrain *Harmony*

Music: JOHN GOSS (1800–1880)

1   See, amid the winter's snow,
      born for us on earth below,
   see, the Lamb of God appears,
      promised from eternal years!

Hail, thou ever-blessèd morn!
   Hail, redemption's happy dawn!
Sing through all Jerusalem:
   Christ is born in Bethlehem!

2   Lo, within a manger lies
      he who built the starry skies,
   he who, throned in height sublime,
      sits amid the cherubim!

* 3   Say, ye holy shepherds, say,
      what your joyful news today;
   wherefore have ye left your sheep
      on the lonely mountain steep?

* 4   'As we watched at dead of night,
      lo, we saw a wondrous light;
   angels, singing "Peace on earth,"
      told us of a Saviour's birth.'

5   Sacred Infant, all divine,
      what a tender love was thine,
   thus to come from highest bliss
      down to such a world as this!

EDWARD CASWALL (1814–1878)*

CALYPSO CAROL

Irregular

See him ly - ing on a bed of straw: a draugh-ty sta - ble with an o - pen door; Ma - ry cra - dl-ing the babe she bore — the Prince of glo - ry is his name.

Refrain

Oh, now car - ry me to Beth-le-hem to see the Lord of love a - gain: just as poor_ as was the

Music: MICHAEL PERRY (1942–1996)
    arranged by ALLAN WICKS (1923–2010)

sta - ble then, _ the Prince of glo - ry when he came!

2   Star of silver, sweep across the skies,
      show where Jesus in the manger lies;
      shepherds, swiftly from your stupor rise
        to see the Saviour of the world!

3   Angels, sing again the song you sang,
      sing the glory of God's gracious plan;
      sing that Bethl'em's little baby can
        be salvation to the soul.

* 4   Mine are riches, from your poverty;
      from your innocence, eternity;
      mine, forgiveness by your death for me,
        child of sorrow for my joy.

MICHAEL PERRY (1942–1996)

QUEM PASTORES   888 7

1   Shepherds came, their praises bringing,
       who had heard the angels singing:
   'Far from you be fear unruly,
      Christ is king of glory born.'

2   Wise men whom a star had guided
       incense, gold, and myrrh provided,
  made their sacrifices truly
     to the king of glory born.

3   Jesus born the king of heaven,
       Christ to us through Mary given,
  to your praise and honour duly
     be resounding glory done.

GEORGE BRADFORD CAIRD (1917–1984)
based on *Quem pastores laudavere*, Latin, 15th century

Music: German 15th-century melody
     adapted by RALPH VAUGHAN WILLIAMS (1872–1958)

STILLE NACHT   Irregular

1   Silent night! Holy night!
      All is calm, all is bright
    round the virgin and her child:
      holy infant so tender and mild,
        sleep in heavenly peace;
        sleep in heavenly peace!

2   Silent night! Holy night!
      Shepherds quail at the sight,
    glory streams from heaven afar,
      heavenly hosts sing 'Alleluia,
        Christ the Saviour is born,
        Christ the Saviour is born!'

3   Silent night! Holy night!
      Son of God, love's pure light:
    radiant beams your holy face
      with the dawn of saving grace,
        Jesus, Lord, at your birth,
        Jesus, Lord, at your birth.

Stille Nacht! Heilige Nacht!
JOSEPH MOHR (1792–1848)
translated by JOHN FREEMAN YOUNG (1820–1885)

Music: Melody by FRANZ XAVER GRUBER (1787–1863)
      arranged by DAVID ILIFF (b. 1939)

1 Sing lul - la - by! Lul - la - by ba - by, now re - -
-clin - ing: sing lul - la - by! Hush, do not wake the in - fant
King; an - gels are watch - ing, stars are shin - ing o - ver the
place where he is ly - ing: sing lul - la - by.
sing lul - la - by.

Music: Basque traditional carol
        arranged by CHARLES EDGAR PETTMAN (1866–1943)

2   Sing lullaby!
Lullaby baby, sweetly sleeping:
   sing lullaby!
Hush, do not wake the infant King;
soon will come sorrow with the morning,
soon will come bitter grief and weeping:
   sing lullaby!

3   Sing lullaby!
Lullaby baby, gently dozing:
   sing lullaby!
Hush, do not wake the infant King;
soon come the cross, the nails, the piercing,
then in the grave at last reposing:
   sing lullaby!

4   Sing lullaby!
Lullaby! Is the baby waking?
   Sing lullaby!
Hush, do not stir the infant King,
dreaming of Easter, gladsome morning,
conquering death, its bondage breaking:
   sing lullaby!

SABINE BARING-GOULD (1834–1924)

Music: Austrian traditional carol
     arranged by MALCOLM ARCHER (*b.* 1952)

1　Still, still, still, the baby lies asleep:
　　yet far away are herald voices —
　　heaven sings, and earth rejoices!
　　Still, still, still, the baby lies asleep.

2　Love, love, love, no greater love than his;
　　while 'Christ the Lord' the angels name him,
　　we with fervent hearts acclaim him.
　　Love, love, love, no greater love than his.

PAUL WIGMORE (1925–2014)
based on *Still, still, still, weil's Kindlein schlafen will*
Austrian carol, modern version
attributed to Johann Gottfried Georg Götsch.

1 Sweet was the song the Vir - gin sang, when she to Beth-lem Ju - da came, and was de - li-vered of _ a _ son, that bless-ed Je - sus hath to name.

Lul - la, lul - la, lul - la-by, _ lul - la, _ lul - la, lul - la-by.

2 'Sweet babe,' sang _ she, 'and eke a Sa - viour born, who hast vouch- -safed from on high to suc-cour _ us, that were for - lorn.'

Lul - la, lul - la, lul - la - by, _ lul - la, _ lul - la, lul - la-by.

Music: MALCOLM ARCHER (*b.* 1952)

3 'Sweet babe,' sang she, and rocked_____ him sweet-ly on her_ knee.

Lul - la - by,_____ lul - la - by. Lul - la, lul - la,

lul - la - by,_____ lul - la, _ lul - la, lul - - la - by.

Anonymous song
in version from William Ballet's lute book, *c.*1590 *

1 The first good joy that Ma - ry had, it was the joy of one; to see the bless - ed Je - sus Christ when he was first her son.

Refrain

* When he was first her son, good man, and bless - ed may he be, both Fa - ther, Son and Ho - ly Ghost, to all e - ter - ni - ty.

* The words for the first line of the Refrain are always taken from the last line of each verse.

Music: English traditional carol
arranged by RICHARD RUNCIMAN TERRY (1865–1938)

1 The first good joy that Mary had,
　　it was the joy of one;
　to see the blessed Jesus Christ
　　when he was first her son;
　　　When he was first her son, good man,
　　　　and blessed may he be,
　　　both Father, Son, and Holy Ghost,
　　　　to all eternity.

2 The next good joy that Mary had,
　　it was the joy of two;
　to see her own son, Jesus Christ,
　　to make the lame to go:

3 The next good joy that Mary had,
　　it was the joy of three;
　to see her own son, Jesus Christ,
　　to make the blind to see:

4 The next good joy that Mary had,
　　it was the joy of four;
　to see her own son, Jesus Christ,
　　to read the Bible o'er:

5 The next good joy that Mary had,
　　it was the joy of five;
　to see her own son, Jesus Christ,
　　to raise the dead to life:

6 The next good joy that Mary had,
　　it was the joy of six;
　to see her own son, Jesus Christ,
　　rise from the crucifix:

7 The next good joy that Mary had,
　　it was the joy of seven;
　to see her own son, Jesus Christ,
　　ascending into heaven:

English folk carol from mediaeval tradition

THE FIRST NOWELL   Irregular

1   The first Nowell the angel did say
     was to Bethlehem's shepherds in fields as they lay;
     in fields where they lay keeping their sheep
     on a cold winter's night that was so deep:

         Nowell, nowell, nowell, nowell,
         born is the King of Israel!

Music: English traditional melody
       arranged by JOHN STAINER (1840–1901)
       from *Christmas Carols New and Old* 1871
       descant by DAVID ILIFF (b. 1939)

Descant (v. 4)

No - - well, ___ no - - well, no - - - - well, no - -

No - - well, ___ no - - well, no - - well, ___ no - -

-well, ___ born is ___ the ___ King of Is - - - ra - el!

-well, ___ born is the King ___ of Is - - - ra - el!

2   Then wise men from a country far
        looked up and saw a guiding star;
    they travelled on by night and day
        to reach the place where Jesus lay:

3   At Bethlehem they entered in,
        on bended knee they worshipped him;
    they offered there in his presence
        their gold and myrrh and frankincense:

4   Then let us all with one accord
        sing praises to our heavenly Lord;
    for Christ has our salvation wrought
        and with his blood our life has bought:

Cornish carol, possibly 18th century
adapted by MICHAEL PERRY (1942–1996)

Music: ALAN RIDOUT (b. 1934)

1 The great God of heaven is come down to earth,
  his mother a virgin, and sinless His birth;
  the Father eternal his Father alone:
  he sleeps in the manger; he reigns on the throne.

   Then let us adore him, and praise his great love:
   to save us poor sinners he came from above.

2 A Babe on the breast of a maiden he lies,
  yet sits with the Father on high in the skies;
  before him their faces the seraphim hide,
  while Joseph stands waiting, unscared, by his side.

3 Lo! here is Emmanuel, here is the child,
  the son that was promised to Mary so mild;
  whose power and dominion shall ever increase,
  the prince that shall rule o'er a kingdom of peace.

4 The Wonderful Counsellor, boundless in might,
  the Father's own image, the beam of his light;
  behold him now wearing the likeness of man,
  weak, helpless, and speechless, in measure a span.

5 O wonder of wonders, which none can unfold:
  the Ancient of Days is an hour or two old;
  the maker of all things is made of the earth,
  man is worshipped by angels, and God comes to birth:

6 The word in the bliss of the Godhead remains,
  yet in flesh comes to suffer the keenest of pains;
  he is that He was, and forever shall be,
  but becomes that he was not, for you and for me.

HENRY RAMSDEN BRAMLEY (1833–1917)

1 The hol-ly and the i-vy when they are both _ full _ grown – of _ all the trees that are in the wood, the _ hol-ly bears the crown. _

Oh, the ri-sing of the _ sun, _ and the run-ning of _ the _ deer, _ the _ play-ing of the mer-ry or-gan, sweet sing-ing in the _ choir!

Music: English traditional carol
harmonised by MALCOLM ARCHER (b. 1952)

1 The holly and the ivy,
       when they are both full grown —
   of all the trees that are in the wood,
       the holly bears the crown.

   Oh, the rising of the sun,
       and the running of the deer,
   the playing of the merry organ,
       sweet singing in the choir!

2 The holly bears a blossom
       as white as any flower;
   and Mary bore sweet Jesus Christ
       to be our sweet Saviour.

3 The holly bears a berry
       as red as any blood;
   and Mary bore sweet Jesus Christ
       to do poor sinners good.

From an English traditional carol,
collected 1911 by Cecil Sharp

LOURDES

11 11 and refrain

Music: Pyrrenean melody, published Grenoble 1882
arranged by MALCOLM ARCHER (*b.* 1952)

1   The mother of Jesus gave birth to her Lord;
the baby she suckles is loved and adored.

Rejoice, rejoice, our Saviour is born!
Rejoice, rejoice, our Saviour is born!

2   The Word of creation, the Lord of all space,
confined as a baby looks up at her face.

3   The King of all peace lies asleep in her care;
and kings kneel in wonder to worship him there.

4   As Lord he will nourish the world with his bread;
yet now by his mother this baby is fed.

5   As Mary with gladness accepted his call,
let us now adore him, the Lord God of all.

SUSAN SAYERS (*b.* 1946)

THE VIRGIN MARY

♩ = 124

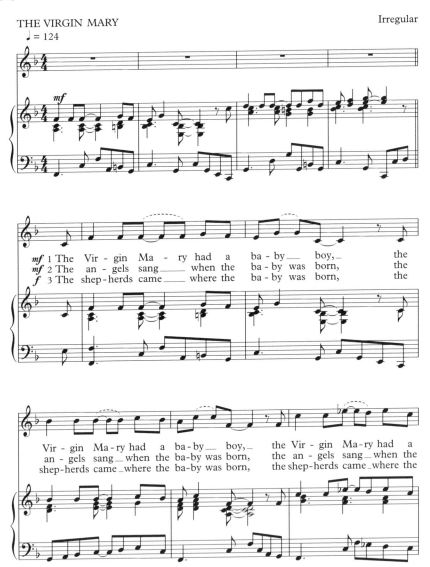

mf 1 The Vir - gin Ma - ry had a ba - by ___ boy, ___ the
mf 2 The an - gels sang ___ when the ba - by was born, the
f 3 The shep - herds came ___ where the ba - by was born, the

Vir - gin Ma - ry had a ba - by ___ boy, ___ the Vir - gin Ma - ry had a
an - gels sang ___ when the ba - by was born, the an - gels sang ___ when the
shep - herds came ___ where the ba - by was born, the shep - herds came ___ where the

Music: West Indian traditional
     as in *The Popular Carol Book*, n.d., Mowbray
     arranged by MALCOLM ARCHER (*b.* 1952)

CHRISTMAS

ba-by__ boy__ and they say that his name is Je - - sus.
ba-by was born and they sang that his name is Je - - sus.
ba-by was born and they say that his name is Je - - sus.

He come from the glo - - ry, he come from the

glo - rious king-dom; he come from the glo - - ry,

he come from the glo - rious king-dom. O

yes, be-liev - er! O yes, be-liev - er! He come from the

glo - ry, he come from the glo - rious king-dom;

CHRISTMAS

West Indian carol

Music: CECIL ARTHUR BROADHURST (1908–1981)
arranged by OLIVER TARNEY (b. 1984)

CHRISTMAS

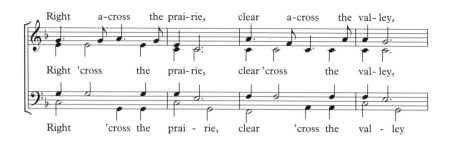

Right a-cross the prai-rie, clear a-cross the val-ley,

Right 'cross the prai-rie, clear 'cross the val-ley,

Right 'cross the prai-rie, clear 'cross the val-ley

straight a-cross the heart of ev-'ry man,

straight 'cross the heart of ev-'ry man, ev-'ry man, there'll be a

straight 'cross the heart of ev-'ry man.

that 'll sweep

right new brand of li-vin' that will sweep like light-nin'

that 'll sweep

Right new brand that will sweep like

f land.

fire, and take a-way the hate from ev-'ry land, ev-'ry land.

fire, and take a-way the

f

Turn for Coda.

There'll be a new world beginnin' from tonight!
There'll be a new world beginnin' from tonight!
  When I climb up to my saddle,
  gonna take him to my heart!
There'll be a new world beginnin' from tonight!

Right across the prairie,
clear across the valley,
straight across the heart of every man,
there'll be a right new brand of livin'
that'll sweep like lightnin' fire,
and take away the hate from every land.

  Yoi, yippee! We're gonna ride the trail!
  Yoi, yippee! We're gonna ride today!
    When I climb up to my saddle,
    gonna take him to my heart!
  There'll be a new world beginnin' from tonight!

CECIL ARTHUR BROADHURST (1908–1981)

1 There's a star in the East on ＿ Christ-mas morn. *Rise up, shep-herd, and*
2 If you take good heed of the an-gels' words.

Oo ＿
Ah ＿ *Rise up, shep-herd, and*

Oo ＿
Ah ＿ *Rise up, shep-herd, and*

Oo ＿
Ah ＿ *Rise up, shep-herd, and*

Rehearsal only

fol-low! It will lead to the place where the Sa-viour's born.
You'll for-get your ＿ flocks, you'll for-get your herds.

fol-low!
oo ＿
ah ＿

fol-low!
oo ＿
ah ＿

fol-low!
oo ＿
ah ＿

Music: African-American spiritual
arranged by MALCOLM ARCHER (b. 1952)

CHRISTMAS

rise up, shep-herd, and fol - low. ____

rise up, shep-herd, and fol - low. ____

rise up, shep-herd, and fol - low. ____

rise up, shep-herd, and fol - low. ____ Leave your sheep, and

Rise up, shep-herd, and fol - low! ____

Rise up, shep-herd, and fol - low! ____

O ____ rise up, shep-herd, and fol - low! ____

leave your lambs. O ____ rise up, shep-herd, and fol - low! ____

CAROLS ANCIENT & MODERN

Leave your ewes and leave your rams. O— rise up shep-herd, and fol - low! —

Rise up shep-herd, and fol - low! —

Rise up shep-herd, and fol - low! —

Rise up shep-herd, and fol - low! —

Fol - low, fol - low. Rise up, shep-herd and fol-low! —

Fol - low, fol - low. Rise up, shep-herd and fol-low! —

Fol - - low, — fol - low. Rise up, shep-herd and fol-low! —

Fol - - low, — fol - low. Rise up, shep-herd and fol-low! —

1   There's a star in the East on Christmas morn.
     Rise up, shepherd, and follow!
   It will lead to the place where the Saviour's born.
     Rise up, shepherd, and follow!

   Leave your sheep and leave your lambs.
     Rise up, shepherd, and follow!
   Leave your ewes and leave your rams.
     Rise up, shepherd, and follow!
   Follow, follow.
     Rise up, shepherd, and follow!
   Follow the Star of Bethlehem.
     Rise up, shepherd, and follow!

2   If you take good heed of the angels' words.
     Rise up, shepherd, and follow!
   You'll forget your flocks, you'll forget your herds.
     Rise up, shepherd, and follow!

African-American spiritual

Music: HECTOR BERLIOZ (1803–1869)

CHRISTMAS

CHRISTMAS

CHRISTMAS

CAROLS ANCIENT & MODERN

safe - ly through the wild! God go with you,

safe - ly through the wild! God go with you,

safe - ly through the wild! God go with you,

safe - ly through the wild! God go with you,

God pro - tect you, guide you safe - ly through the

God pro - tect you, guide you safe - ly through the

God pro - tect you, guide you safe - ly through the

God pro - tect you, guide you safe - ly through the

1 Thou must leave thy lowly dwelling,
   the humble crib, the stable bare,
babe, all mortal babes excelling,
   content our earthly lot to share.
Loving father, loving mother,
   shelter thee with tender care!

2 Blessed Jesus, we implore thee
   with humble love and holy fear,
in the land that lies before thee,
   forget not us who linger here!
May the shepherd's lowly calling,
   ever to thy heart be dear!

3 Blest are ye beyond all measure,
   thou happy father, mother mild!
Guard ye well your heav'nly treasure,
   the Prince of Peace, the Holy Child!
God go with you, God protect you,
   guide you safely through the wild!

HECTOR BERLIOZ (1803–1869)
translated by PAUL ENGLAND (*c.*1863–1932)

FRAGRANCE

Music: French traditional melody
    harmonised by PETER MOGER (*b.* 1964)

1   Thou who wast rich beyond all splendour,
    all for love's sake becamest poor;
thrones for a manger didst surrender,
    sapphire-paved courts for stable floor.
Thou who wast rich beyond all splendour,
    all for love's sake becamest poor.

2   Thou who art God beyond all praising,
    all for love's sake becamest man;
stooping so low, but sinners raising
    heavenwards by thine eternal plan.
Thou who art God beyond all praising,
    all for love's sake becamest man.

3   Thou who art love beyond all telling,
    Saviour and King, we worship thee.
Emmanuel, within us dwelling,
    make us what thou wouldst have us be.
Thou who art love, beyond all telling,
    Saviour and King, we worship thee.

FRANK HOUGHTON (1894–1972)

e - - ia,   e - - ia,

Music: Kölner Psalter, 1638
arranged by MARTIN SHAW (1875–1958)

1　To us in Bethle'm city
　　　was born a little son;
　in him all gentle graces
　　　were gathered into one,
　　　　eia, eia,
　　　were gathered into one.

2　And all our love and fortune
　　　lie in his mighty hands;
　our sorrows, joys and failures
　　　he sees and understands,
　　　　eia, eia,
　　　he sees and understands.

3　O Shepherd, ever near us,
　　　we'll go where thou dost lead;
　no matter where the pasture,
　　　with thee at hand to feed,
　　　　eia, eia,
　　　with thee at hand to feed.

4　No grief shall part us from thee,
　　　however shard the edge:
　we'll serve, and do thy bidding —
　　　O take our hearts in pledge!
　　　　eia, eia,
　　　O take our hearts in pledge!

CECIL ARMSTRONG GIBBS (1889–1960)
based on *Zu Bethlehem geboren*
in *Kölner Psalter,* 1638

Sing, O my love! O my love, my love, my love; this have I done for my true love.

1   Tomorrow shall be my dancing day;
        I would my true love did so chance
    to see the legend of my play,
        to call my true love to my dance;

        Sing, O my love! O my love, my love, my love;
            this have I done for my true love.

2   Then was I born of a virgin pure,
        of her I took fleshly substance;
    thus was I knit to man's nature,
        to call my true love to my dance.

Music: English carol melody in Sandys's
    Christmas Carols Ancient and Modern, 1833
    arranged by RICHARD RUNCIMAN TERRY (1865–1938)

3 In a manger laid, and wrapped I was,
  so very poor, this was my chance,
 betwixt an ox and a silly poor ass,
  to call my true love to my dance.

4 Then afterwards baptized I was,
  the Holy Ghost on me did glance,
 my Father's voice heard from above,
  to call my true love to my dance.

5 Into the desert I was led,
  where I fasted without substance;
 the devil bade me make stones my bread,
  to have me break my true love's dance.

6 The Jews on me they make great suit,
  and with me made great variance,
 because they loved darkness rather than light
  to call my true love to my dance.

7 For thirty pence Judas me sold,
  his covetousness for to advance;
 mark whom I kiss, the same do hold,
  The same is he shall lead the dance.

8 Before Pilate the Jews me brought,
  where Barabbas had deliverance;
 they scourged me and set me at nought,
  judged me to die to lead the dance.

9 Then on the cross hangèd I was,
  where a spear my heart did glance;
 there issued forth both water and blood,
  to call my true love to my dance.

10 Then down to hell I took my way
  for my true love's deliverance,
 and rose again on the third day,
  up to my true love to the dance.

11 Then up to heaven I did ascend,
  where now I dwell in sure substance,
 on the right hand of God, that man
  may come unto the general dance.

English traditional carol in Sandys's *Christmas Carols
Ancient and Modern*, 1833

Music: JOHN JOUBERT (*b.* 1927)

97   Music: © Novello, Chester Music and Novello & Co, 14-15 Berners Street, London W1T 3LJ   UK

CHRISTMAS

CHRISTMAS

Galician carol *Vilancico de Navidad*
translated by JOHN BRANDE TREND (1887–1958)

Man.

f Full

1 Un-to us is born a Son, King of quires su-per-nal: see on earth his

Ped.

life be-gun, of lords the Lord e - ter - nal, of lords the Lord e-ter - nal.

* Voices unaccompanied

S, A *mf*

2 Christ, from heav'n de-scend-ing low, — comes on earth a stran - ger; —

T, B

mf

* May be sung unaccompanied, or by unison voices and organ.

Music: Melody in *Piae Cantiones*, 1582
     arranged by DAVID WILLCOCKS (1919–2015)

CHRISTMAS

ox and ass their own - er know, be - cra - dled in the __

man - - ger, be - cra - dled in the man - - ger.

Tenors and Basses

3 This did He - rod sore af - fray, and grie - vous - ly be -

Full Sw. *mf*

Ped.

-wild - er; so he gave the word to slay, and slew the lit - tle

Man.

child - - er, and slew the lit - tle child - er.

Sopranos

4 Of his love and mer - cy mild this the Christ - mas sto - - ry and O that Ma - ry's gen - tle Child might lead us up to glo - ry, might lead us up to glo - ry.

CHRISTMAS

* optional, or soprano part as a descant.

Do - mi - no, be - ne - di - ca - mus Do - mi - no.

Do - mi - no, be - ne - di - ca - mus Do - mi - no.

1   Unto us is born a Son,
        King of quires supernal:
    see on earth his life begun,
        of lords the Lord eternal,
        of lords the Lord eternal.

2   Christ, from heav'n descending low,
        comes on earth a stranger;
    ox and ass their owner know,
        becradled in the manger,
        becradled in the manger.

3   This did Herod sore affray,
        and grievously bewilder;
    so he gave the word to slay,
        and slew the little childer,
        and slew the little childer.

4   Of his love and mercy mild
        this the Christmas story;
    and O that Mary's gentle child
        might lead us up to glory,
        might lead us up to glory!

5   O and A, and A and O,
        cum cantibus in choro,
    let our merry organ go,
        benedicamus Domino,
        benedicamus Domino.

Puer nobis nascitur in *Piae Cantiones,* 1582
translated by GEORGE RATCLIFFE WOODWARD (1848–1934)

Music: English traditional carol
arranged by JOHN BARNARD (*b.* 1948)

3 For we all like figgy pud-ding, we all like figgy pud-ding, we all like figgy pud-ding, so bring some out here!

4 For we won't go un-til we've got some, we won't go un-til we've got some, we won't go un-til we've got some, so bring some out here! Good ti-dings we bring to you and your kin; we wish you a mer-ry Christ-mas and a hap-py New Year.

English traditional *envoi* carol

GREENSLEEVES   87 87 68 67

Music: English traditional melody
    arranged by MALCOLM ARCHER (b. 1952)

1   What child is this, who, laid to rest
        on Mary's lap is sleeping?
    whom angels greet with anthems sweet,
        while shepherds watch are keeping?
        this, this is Christ the King,
    whom shepherds worship and angels sing:
        haste, haste to bring him praise
    the babe, the son of Mary.

2   Why lies he in such mean estate,
        where ox and ass are feeding?
    Come, have no fear, God's Son is here,
        his love all loves exceeding:
        nails, spear, shall pierce him through,
    the cross be borne for me, for you:
        hail, hail, the Saviour comes,
    the babe, the son of Mary.

3   So bring him incense, gold and myrrh,
        all tongues and peoples own him,
    the King of kings salvation brings,
        let every heart enthrone him:
        raise, raise your song on high
    while Mary sings a lullaby,
        joy, joy, for Christ is born,
    the babe, the son of Mary.

WILLIAM CHATTERTON DIX (1837–1898)
and Compilers of *New English Hymnal,* 1986

QUELLE EST CETTE ODEUR   98 98 98

Music: Early 18th-century melody, known in England and in France
arranged by MALCOLM ARCHER (*b.* 1952)

1   Whence is the goodly fragrance flowing,
        stealing our senses all away?
    Never the like did come a-blowing,
        shepherds, in flow'ry fields of May.
    Whence is that goodly fragrance flowing,
        stealing our senses all away?

2   What is that light so brilliant, breaking
        here in the night across our eyes?
    Never so bright, the day-star waking,
        started to climb the morning skies!
    What is that light so brilliant, breaking,
        here in the night across our eyes?

3   Bethlehem! there in manger lying,
        find your Redeemer haste away.
    Run ye with eager footsteps vieing,
        worship the Saviour born today.
    Bethlehem! there in manger lying,
        find your Redeemer haste away.

Quelle est cette odeur agréable
Late 17th-century French poem
translated by ALLEN BEVILLE RAMSAY (1872–1955)

WINCHESTER OLD CM

Music: Ascribed to GEORGE KIRBYE (*c.*1565–1634)
in Thomas Este's *The whole booke of psalmes,* 1592
Possibly derived from Christopher Tye's *The Actes of the Apostles,* 1553
descant by ALAN GRAY (1855–1935)

1   While shepherds watched their flocks by night,
      all seated on the ground,
the angel of the Lord came down,
      and glory shone around.

2   'Fear not,' said he (for mighty dread
      had seized their troubled mind);
'glad tidings of great joy I bring
      to you and all mankind.

3   'To you in David's town this day
      is born of David's line
a Saviour, who is Christ the Lord;
      and this shall be the sign:

4   'the heavenly babe you there shall find
      to human view displayed,
all meanly wrapped in swathing bands,
      and in a manger laid.'

5   Thus spake the seraph; and forthwith
      appeared a shining throng
of angels praising God, who thus
      addressed their joyful song:

6   'All glory be to God on high,
      and to the earth be peace;
good will henceforth from heaven to men
      begin and never cease.'

NAHUM TATE (1652–1715)
based on Luke 2.1-20

CRANBROOK   Irregular

1 While shep-herds watched their flocks by night, all seat-ed on the ground, the an-gel of the Lord came down, the an-gel of the Lord came down, and glo-ry shone a-round, and glo-ry shone a-round, (a-round,) and glo-ry shone a-round.

Music: THOMAS CLARK (1775–1859)
       arranged by DAVID PEACOCK (b. 1949)

1   While shepherds watched their flocks by night,
      all seated on the ground,
  the angel of the Lord came down,
      and glory shone around.

2   'Fear not,' said he (for mighty dread
      had seized their troubled mind);
  'glad tidings of great joy I bring
      to you and all mankind.

3   'To you in David's town this day
      is born of David's line
  a Saviour, who is Christ the Lord;
      and this shall be the sign:

4   'the heavenly babe you there shall find
      to human view displayed,
  all meanly wrapped in swathing bands,
      and in a manger laid.'

5   Thus spake the seraph; and forthwith
      appeared a shining throng
  of angels praising God, who thus
      addressed their joyful song:

6   'All glory be to God on high,
      and to the earth be peace;
  good will henceforth from heaven to men
      begin and never cease.'

NAHUM TATE (1652–1715)
based on Luke 2.1-20

SCARLET RIBBONS   87 87 D

Music: EVELYN DANZIG (1901–1996)
    arranged by JOHN L. BELL (b. 1949)

1   Who would think that what was needed
     to transform and save the earth
might not be a plan or army
     proud in purpose, proved in worth?
Who would think, despite derision,
     that a child should lead the way?
God surprises earth with heaven,
     coming here on Christmas Day.

2   Shepherds watch and wise men wonder,
     monarchs scorn and angels sing;
such a place as none would reckon
     hosts a holy, helpless thing;
stabled beasts and bypassed strangers
     watch a baby laid in hay:
God surprises earth with heaven,
     coming here on Christmas Day.

3   Centuries of skill and science
     span the past from which we move,
yet experience questions whether
     with such progress we improve.
While the human lot we ponder,
     lest our hopes and humour fray,
God surprises earth with heaven,
     coming here on Christmas Day.

JOHN L. BELL (b. 1949)
and GRAHAM MAULE (b. 1958)

103 Words: From *Heaven Shall Not Wait*, 1987. © 1987, WGRG, c/o Iona Community, Glasgow G5 9JP Scotland.
<www.wildgoose.scot> All rights reserved. Used by permission.

EPIPHANY

DIX   77 77 77

*When the descant is **not** used, the harmonies for lines 1 and 2
may be repeated for lines 3 and 4.*

Music: From a chorale by CONRAD KOCHER (1786–1872)
         abridged by WILLIAM HENRY MONK (1823–1889)
         descant by SYDNEY HUGO NICHOLSON (1875–1947)

EPIPHANY

1   As with gladness men of old
        did the guiding star behold,
    as with joy they hailed its light,
        leading onward, beaming bright;
        so, most gracious Lord, may we
        evermore be led to thee.

2   As with joyful steps they sped,
        Saviour, to thy lowly bed,
    there to bend the knee before
        thee whom heaven and earth adore;
        so may we with willing feet
        ever seek thy mercy-seat.

3   As they offered gifts most rare
        at thy cradle rude and bare,
    so may we with holy joy,
        pure and free from sin's alloy,
        all our costliest treasures bring,
        Christ, to thee our heavenly King.

4   Holy Jesus, every day
        keep us in the narrow way,
    and, when earthly things are past,
        bring our ransomed souls at last
        where they need no star to guide,
        where no clouds thy glory hide.

5   In the heavenly country bright
        need they no created light;
    thou its light, its joy, its crown,
        thou its sun which goes not down;
        there for ever may we sing
        alleluias to our King.

WILLIAM CHATTERTON DIX (1837–1898)

STUTTGART

87 87

Music: Melody probably by Christian Friedrich Witt (*c.*1660–1717)
in *Psalmodia Sacra,* Gotha, 1715
Adapted 1861 by Henry John Gauntlett (1805–1876)
Harmony as in *English Hymnal,* 1906

1   Bethlehem, of noblest cities
       none can once with thee compare;
    thou alone the Lord from heaven
       didst for us incarnate bear.

2   Fairer than the sun at morning
       was the star that told his birth;
    to the lands their God announcing,
       seen in fleshly form on earth.

3   By its lambent beauty guided
       see the eastern kings appear;
    see them bend, their gifts to offer,
       gifts of incense, gold and myrrh.

4   Solemn things of mystic meaning:
       incense doth the God disclose,
    gold a royal child proclaimeth,
       myrrh a future tomb foreshows.

5   Holy Jesu, by thy brightness
       to the Gentile world displayed,
    with the Father and the Spirit
       endless praise to thee be paid.

AURELIUS CLEMENS PRUDENTIUS (348–.413)
translated by EDWARD CASWALL (1814–1878)

EPIPHANY

11 10 11 10

Music: Joseph Francis Thrupp (1827–1867)

106 ii

WESSEX

11 10 11 10

Music: ALWYN SURPLICE (1906–1977)

1   Brightest and best of the sons of the morning,
        dawn on our darkness, and lend us thine aid;
    star of the east, the horizon adorning,
        guide where our infant Redeemer is laid.

2   Cold on his cradle the dew-drops are shining;
        low lies his head with the beasts of the stall;
    angels adore him in slumber reclining,
        Maker and Monarch and Saviour of all.

3   Say, shall we yield him, in costly devotion,
        odours of Edom, and offerings divine,
    gems of the mountain, and pearls of the ocean,
        myrrh from the forest, or gold from the mine?

4   Vainly we offer each ample oblation,
        vainly with gifts would his favour secure:
    richer by far is the heart's adoration,
        dearer to God are the prayers of the poor.

5   Brightest and best of the sons of the morning,
        dawn on our darkness, and lend us thine aid;
    star of the east, the horizon adorning,
        guide where our infant Redeemer is laid.

REGINALD HEBER (1783–1826)

PASTOR PASTORUM   65 65

Music: Tune set to *Alle Jahre wieder kommt das Christuskind*
in his *Dreistimmiges Württembergisches Choralbuch,*
by PHILIPP FRIEDRICH SILCHER (1789–1860)

1   Faithful vigil ended,
      watching, waiting cease;
   Master, grant your servant
      his discharge in peace.

2   All the Spirit promised,
      all the Father willed,
   now these eyes behold it
      perfectly fulfilled.

3   This your great deliverance
      sets your people free;
   Christ their light uplifted
      all the nations see.

4   Christ, your people's glory!
      Watching, doubting cease:
   grant to us your servants
      our discharge in peace.

TIMOTHY DUDLEY-SMITH (*b.* 1926)
based on Luke 2.29-32
(Nunc Dimittis, The Song of Simeon)

UPTON CHEYNEY

74 74 D

Music: JOHN BARNARD (b. 1948)

EPIPHANY

1   In our darkness light has shone,
      Alleluia,
   still today the light shines on,
      Alleluia;
   Word made flesh in human birth,
      Alleluia,
   Light and Life of all the earth,
      Alleluia!

2   Christ the Son incarnate see,
      Alleluia,
   by whom all things came to be,
      Alleluia;
   through the world his splendours shine,
      Alleluia,
   full of grace and truth divine,
      Alleluia!

3   All who now in him believe,
      Alleluia,
   everlasting life receive,
      Alleluia;
   born of God and in his care,
      Alleluia,
   we his name and nature share,
      Alleluia!

4   Christ a child on earth appears,
      Alleluia,
   crown of all creation's years,
      Alleluia;
   God's eternal Word has come,
      Alleluia,
   he shall lead his people home,
      Alleluia!

TIMOTHY DUDLEY-SMITH (b. 1926)
based on John 1.1-14

WAS LEBET

Music: Melody from *Rheinhardt MS,* 1754

1   O worship the Lord in the beauty of holiness;
      bow down before him, his glory proclaim;
    with gold of obedience, and incense of lowliness,
      kneel and adore him: the Lord is his name.

2   Low at his feet lay thy burden of carefulness:
      high on his heart he will bear it for thee,
    comfort thy sorrows, and answer thy prayerfulness,
      guiding thy steps as may best for thee be.

3   Fear not to enter his courts in the slenderness
      of the poor wealth thou wouldst reckon as thine:
    truth in its beauty, and love in its tenderness,
      these are the offerings to lay on his shrine.

4   These, though we bring them in trembling and fearfulness,
      he will accept for the name that is dear;
    mornings of joy give for evenings of tearfulness,
      trust for our trembling and hope for our fear.

5   O worship the Lord in the beauty of holiness;
      bow down before him, his glory proclaim;
    with gold of obedience, and incense of lowliness,
      kneel and adore him: the Lord is his name.

JOHN SAMUEL BEWLEY MONSELL (1811–1875)

1 One star shone a-cross the east-ern sky;

One star shone up-on a watch-ful eye.

Music: MALCOLM ARCHER (*b.* 1952)

EPIPHANY

And for a mil- lion mil-lion years or more this star had shone that way be-fore, but on this night _____ this star shone

bright____ and there, a - mazed,____ the Ma-gi saw   a

star   de - fy-ing na-ture's law.____   One

EPIPHANY

star.

Ah _____

mp Soprano (and Alto)

mp Tenor, Bass

2 One star tra-vel-ling a-cross the dawn!

mf

mp

Ah _____

One star tell-ing them a child is born,

Ah

cresc.

and then im - plor-ing them to start their quest, to

cresc.

_mp_

Ah

fol - low on from east to west a-cross the wild _____ to find a

_f_

_mf_

Ah

child: _____ the God of all _____ up-on this earth, a

EPIPHANY

EPIPHANY

CAROLS ANCIENT & MODERN

EPIPHANY

1   One star
shone across the eastern sky;
   one star
shone upon a watchful eye:
and for a million million years or more
this star had shone that way before,
   but on this night
   this star shone bright
and there, amazed, the Magi saw
a star defying nature's law.

2   One star
travelling across the dawn!
   One star
telling them a child is born
and then imploring them to start their quest
to follow on from east to west
   across the wild
   to find a child,
the God of all upon this earth,
a baby boy by human birth.

3   One Star
lying at his mother's breast;
   one Star
brighter far than all the rest:
and for a million million years or more
no Star had shone like this before.
   From far above
   he came with love
and Christ our Saviour led the way
and taught us how to love today.

PAUL WIGMORE (1925–2014)

ST EDMUND   77 77 D

1   Songs of thankfulness and praise,
     Jesu, Lord, to thee we raise,
manifested by the star
     to the sages from afar;
branch of royal David's stem
     in thy birth at Bethlehem:
anthems be to thee addrest,
     God in man made manifest.

Music: CHARLES STEGGALL (1826–1905)

2   Manifest at Jordan's stream,
      Prophet, Priest, and King supreme;
    and at Cana wedding-guest
      in thy Godhead manifest;
    manifest in power divine,
      changing water into wine:
    anthems be to thee addrest,
      God in man made manifest.

3   Manifest in making whole
      palsied limbs and fainting soul;
    manifest in valiant fight,
      quelling all the devil's might;
    manifest in gracious will,
      ever bringing good from ill:
    anthems be to thee addrest,
      God in man made manifest.

* 4   Sun and moon shall darkened be,
      stars shall fall, the heavens shall flee;
    Christ will then like lightning shine,
      all will see his glorious sign;
    all will then the trumpet hear,
      all will see the Judge appear:
    thou by all wilt be confest,
      God in man made manifest.

5   Grant us grace to see thee, Lord,
      mirrored in thy holy word;
    may we imitate thee now,
      and be pure, as pure art thou;
    that we like to thee may be
      at thy great Epiphany;
    and may praise thee, ever blest,
      God in man made manifest.

CHRISTOPHER WORDSWORTH (1807–1885)

* The singers would be placed, if possible, at some distance from the soloist.

Music: Chorale melody by PHILIPP NICOLAI (1556–1608)
    adapted by PETER CORNELIUS (1824–1874)
    arranged by IVOR ATKINS (1869–1953)

E P I P H A N Y

new-born King of the Jews may be. Full roy-al gifts they bear for the

truth   from   heav'n   a - - far   our

truth   from   heav'n   a - far   our

King; gold, in - cense, myrrh are their of - fer - ing.   2 The star shines

Jes - - se   tree__ now   blow - - - eth.

Jes - - se   tree   now   blow - - - eth.

EPIPHANY

CAROLS ANCIENT & MODERN

EPIPHANY

-place. Gold, in-cense, myrrh thou canst not bring; of-fer thy heart __ to the

life   be - stow - - - - ing. _____ Praise, O _

life   be - - stow - - - - ing. Praise, O _ praise, praise, O _

life   be - - stow - - - - ing. _____ Praise, O _

life   be - - stow - - - - ing. ____ Praise, O

1   Three Kings from Persian lands afar
to Jordan follow the pointing star:
and this the quest of the travellers three,
where the new-born King of the Jews may be.
Full royal gifts they bear for the King;
gold, incense, myrrh are their offering.

> *How brightly shines the morning star!*
> *With grace and truth from heaven afar*
> *our Jesse tree now bloweth.*

2   The star shines out with a steadfast ray;
the kings to Bethlehem make their way,
and there in worship they bend the knee,
as Mary's child in her lap they see;
their royal gifts they show to the King;
gold, incense, myrrh are their offering.

> *Of Jacob's stem and David's line,*
> *for thee, my Bridegroom, King divine,*
> *my soul with love o'erfloweth.*

3   Thou child of man, lo, to Bethlehem
the Kings are travelling, travel with them!
The star of mercy, the star of grace,
shall lead thy heart to its resting place.
Gold, incense, myrrh thou canst not bring;
offer thy heart to the infant King.

> *Thy word, Jesu, inly feeds us,*
> *rightly leads us, life bestowing.*
> *Praise, O praise such love o'erflowing.*

Drei Kön'ge wandern aus Morgenland
PETER CORNELIUS (1824–1874)
translated by HERBERT NEWELL BATE (1871–1941)
Based loosely on *Wie schön leuchtet der Morgenstern*
by PHILIPP NICOLAI (1556–1608)

THREE KINGS OF ORIENT   88 86 and refrain

Music: EDWARD JOHN HOPKINS (1818–1901)

1 We three kings of Orient are,
     bearing gifts we traverse afar
field and fountain, moor and mountain,
     following yonder star:

> *O star of wonder, star of night,*
> *star with royal beauty bright,*
> *westward leading, still proceeding,*
> *guide us to thy perfect light.*

2 Born a king on Bethlehem plain,
     gold I bring to crown him again,
king for ever, ceasing never
     over us all to reign:

3 Frankincense to offer have I,
     incense owns a deity nigh;
prayer and praising, all men raising,
     worship him, God most high:

4 Myrrh is mine, its bitter perfume
     breathes a life of gathering gloom;
sorrowing, sighing, bleeding, dying,
     sealed in the stone-cold tomb:

5 Glorious now behold him arise,
     king and God and sacrifice.
Heaven sings: 'Alleluia';
     'Alleluia,' the earth replies:

EDWARD JOHN HOPKINS (1818–1901)*

CHRISTINGLE

FALLING FIFTHS   7775 775

God whose love is ev-ery-where _ made our earth and all things fair, _ ev-er keeps them in his care; _ praise the God of love! He who hung the stars in space holds the spin-ning world in place; praise the God of love!

Fine   *Optional link*   *D.C.*

Music: NOËL TREDINNICK (*b.* 1949)

CHRISTINGLE

2   Come with thankfulness to sing
of the gifts the seasons bring,
summer, winter, autumn, spring;
   praise the God of love!
He who gave us breath and birth
gives us all the fruitful earth;
   praise the God of love!

3   Mark what love the Lord displayed,
all our sins upon him laid,
by his blood our ransom paid;
   praise the God of love!
Circled by that scarlet band
all the world is in his hand;
   praise the God of love!

4   See the sign of love appear,
flame of glory, bright and clear,
light for all the world is here;
   praise the God of love!
Gloom and darkness, get you gone!
Christ the Light of life has shone;
   praise the God of love!

TIMOTHY DUDLEY-SMITH (b. 1926)

114 Words: © Timothy Dudley-Smith in Europe and Africa; © Hope Publishing Company for the United States of America and the rest of world. Reproduced by permission of Oxford University Press. All rights reserved.

THE HOLLY AND THE IVY   76 87 and refrain

1 It's round-ed like an o-range, this earth on which we stand; and we

praise the God who holds it in the hol-low of his hand.

So Fa-ther we would thank you for all that you have done, and for

all that you have giv-en us through the com-ing of your Son.

Music: English traditional carol
  harmonised by MALCOLM ARCHER (b. 1952)

2   A candle, burning brightly,
        can cheer the darkest night,
    and these candles tell how Jesus
        came to bring a dark world light.

3   The ribbon round the orange
        reminds us of the cost;
    how the Shepherd, strong and gentle,
        gave his life to save the lost.

4   Four seasons with their harvest
        supply the food we need,
    and the Spirit gives a harvest
        that can make us rich indeed.

5   We come with our Christingles
        to tell of Jesus' birth,
    and we praise the God who blessed us
        by his coming to this earth.

BASIL BRIDGE (b. 1927)

Music: Popular American melody
arranged by ANNE HARRISON (*b.* 1954)

CHRISTINGLE

let it shine, let it shine, let it shine.

Fine
Pause last time only
to Verses

The light that shines is the light of love,
On Mon-day he gave me the gift of love,

Fine

lights the dark-ness from a - bove. It shines on me and it
Tues- day, peace came from a - bove. On Wednes-day he told me to

shines on you,___ and shows what the pow-er of___
have more faith,___ on Thurs-day he gave me a

love___ can do. I'm gon-na shine my___ light___ both___
lit-tle more grace.___ Fri-day, he told me just to

far and near,___ I'm gon-na shine___ my___ light both___
watch and pray,___ Sa-tur-day, he told me just

CHRISTINGLE

bright and clear. _ Where there's a dark _ cor - ner _
what to say. _ On Sun - day he gave me the

D.C. al Fine

in this land _ I'm gon-na let my lit-tle light shine.
power di - vine _ to let my lit-tle light shine.

possibly based on a song by HARRY DIXON LOES (1895–1965)

INDEXES

INDEX of COMPOSERS, ARRANGERS
and SOURCES of MELODIES

INDEX of AUTHORS, TRANSLATORS
and SOURCES of WORDS

INDEX of FIRST LINES and TITLES
(Names in parentheses are alternative titles.)